Startup Cafe

Stories from Silicon Valley and beyond

Bill Rollinson

Crystal Cove Press

Startup Cafe

CONTENTS

1. Introduction — 1
2. Chapter 1 - Go West — 4
3. Chapter 2 - The Heart of the Valley — 9
4. Chapter 3 - Coast to Coast — 21
5. Chapter 4 - Return to the Valley — 32
6. Chapter 5 - A Garage in Atherton — 57
7. Chapter 6 - The Unfortunate Cake Disaster — 81
8. Chapter 7 - Time for a Real Job — 101
9. Chapter 8 - The Great Relocation — 118
10. Chapter 9 - Another Startup? — 121
11. Chapter 10 - Lessons Learned — 123
12. Acknowledgments — 127
13. About the Author — 129

Copyright © 2022 by Bill Rollinson

All rights reserved. No part of this book may be reproduced in any manner whatsoever without written permission except in the case of brief quotations embodied in critical articles and reviews.

First Printing, 2022

1

Introduction

"For what it's worth: it's never too late, or in my case, too early to be whoever you want to be. There's no time limit, stop whenever you want. You can change, or stay the same, there are no rules to this thing. We can make the best or worst of it. I hope you make the best of it. And I hope you see things that startle you. I hope you feel things you have never felt before. I hope you meet people with a different point of view. I hope you live a life that you are proud of. If you're not, I hope you have the courage to start over again."

- **F Scott Fitzgerald**

When I saw the above quote from F Scott Fitzgerald simply framed in a tiny guest bathroom in a writer's home in Palo Alto, I knew I had to include it at the very beginning of this book. I started to think seriously about writing this book more than 30 years ago. I was early in my career, newly married and had just started a business in downtown Palo Alto at 236 Hamilton Ave. in the heart of Silicon Valley. I began my graphic design business above Caffe Verona in Palo Alto in 1984 just as the Apple Macintosh computer was being introduced. Our team was lucky enough to help develop and launch ClickArt, the fifth software program available for the Mac. Originally a drive-through feed and fuel business, Caffe Verona became a popular meeting spot. Jim Clark first met Marc Andressen at the cafe at 7:30 in the morning in early 1994. Shortly afterward, the two would found Netscape Communications Corporation.

People say that writing a book is hard, takes more time than you ever think, and most people who start, never finish. Well I want to finish what I started so long ago. The good (and bad) news is that I have a lot more material to write about.

Originally, I thought that Startup Cafe would be a way to share what it has meant to live and work in the San Francisco Bay Area for the past 50+ years, starting in 1967 and how it feels to make the transition from an entrepreneur to a full time employee at Google.

Then, in the midst of my writing, a global pandemic hit in March of 2020, and created uncertainty around the way we live and work. In August, 2020, my wife and I moved 2800 miles away from Silicon Valley to Raleigh, North Carolina. Fully remote, hybrid, and flexibility are all the new buzz words.

My one simple goal is to help people who are contemplating a big change, like becoming an entrepreneur, by giving them the courage and tools to start that incredible journey, and build something new.

STARTUP CAFE

2

Chapter 1 - Go West

The building shook. Suddenly all of the computers in the office died. My small business in Palo Alto was five years old and everyone was out in the street wondering what to do next. The San Francisco Bay Area had just experienced the Loma Prieta earthquake.

Carol from the cafe below our office was screaming hysterically, as she was deathly afraid of aftershocks. I grabbed my bike and got everyone outside as quickly as possible. Since my house was close by, I often rode my bike to and from work. On this day, I happened to have my car parked below the Palo Alto City Hall. No way was I going near the underground parking structure after the earthquake. I slowly peddled home.

So does your physical location really matter when you start a business? The answer is not that simple, especially in light of the recent Covid pandemic outbreak that has forever shifted how and where we choose to work.

I had the amazing luck to end up in the San Francisco Bay Area all because my dad, Bruce, was transferring to his company's "home" office in San Francisco and my mom, sister and I were all going along for the ride.

As I look back, I have my dad to thank for planting the seed that would become my later interest both in the creative field of design and also an interest in computers. My dad was working in sales for a company called TAB Products that made accessories for computers and because he was in Northern New Jersey he was calling on Bell Labs and other new and growing concerns that were adding computers in the late 1960's. TAB was founded by two ex-IBMers, Harry LeClaire and Si Foote,who both saw the need for a whole line of equipment to support the growing demand from businesses as they added the giant computing machines to their offices. The theme of people leaving a large company like IBM and starting something brand new would be something I witnessed over and over again, especially out in California.

Another interesting theme that I also noticed early on was that many tech founders really liked spending time in Napa Valley. "Si" Foote could have easily been one of the first to start this trend. He and his wife were the founders of the Land Trust of Napa County and towering figures in Napa County conservation. From 1976, until his move to Oregon in 1995, Si served as a board member, president, donor, land donor and advisory council member of the Land Trust. Without Foote and his wife June, there would not be a land trust in Napa County as we know it today. Shortly after graduating from the University of California, Berkeley, Foote started TAB Products with partner Harry Le Claire. They patented the vertical filing cabinet that is now ubiquitous in medical offices (the dentist office I go to still uses TAB cabinets today!) Foote and his wife retired in the 1970's and moved to Napa County, where they built a stone house overlooking the Silverado Trail near Yountville. The stones used to build the house came from the Napa River and Si and June labored to pick and carry many of the individual stones themselves. The house they built in 1971 was not just any vineyard property, but one that comes with 360 degree views that stretch, literally, as far as the eye can see. The 6,000 square foot, stone and glass, one bedroom two bath main house has windows all around and a pool perched on one side of the knoll. Adjacent to it is a two bedroom guest house so you don't go about tripping over awakening guests (who might have spent a bit too long sipping wine late into the night) while you have your breakfast in the main house, or on one of the landscaped patios, perhaps beneath a persimmon tree. The pool was for June who needed to swim daily because of her bad back. Si once told a friend, that "Rich people don't realize that giving away money is much more fun than making it." By establishing the Land Trust, he and June set an example in the county of removing a percentage of land from development and helping to maintain the rural feel and the farming land in Napa County.

During this time there was a popular soft drink called "TAB" and when people asked where my dad worked and I said "TAB" they would always assume it was for the soft drink company. Very few people worked in the computer industry. The Coca-Cola Company introduced Tab in 1963 as Coca-Cola's first diet drink, Tab was notably popular throughout the 1960s and 1970s.

Being all of eight years old when we moved to Northern California, I had little interest or memory of how we decided to settle in the hills of San Carlos on the border of Belmont. Our house in the hills was new and about 30 minutes south of San Francisco (today that same commute takes almost triple the time for the same distance, because of the traffic). We had fantastic views - from the San Mateo Bridge (built in 1961) all the way to San Francisco from the decks that wrapped around the front of the house. The only drawback to hanging out on the decks were the severe winds that would come up from the flat lands and make spending any length of time outside nearly impossible, and for an eight year old, downright dangerous.

One of the best parts of where we lived was the freedom it afforded. Our house backed up to the hills above Carlmont High School that was full of dirt trails and an amazing amount of poison oak that a kid from the East Coast had no clue about. Soon after we moved in I remember trying to rescue a kite from a bush with almost no leaves. No big deal. Until a day later all my exposed skin had a severe case of poison oak. Lesson learned. The street we lived on was a dead end, so bike riding, skateboarding and just fooling around doing kid stuff was easy, as the neighborhood kids controlled the streets. We explored the hills, built forts and really didn't have much to worry about, except getting home in time for dinner.

Another benefit of our location was that there was a high school right below our house and it allowed us the freedom to walk the trails and use some of the athletic facilities of the school. I ended up playing tennis at a time when the sport wasn't that popular and the courts were usually empty. I remember taking a Judo class at the high school. Being able to use the trails to get down to the high school was important because the roads leading down were too steep to ride a bike and outright dangerous (as I grew older I did attempt to ride my bike up and down the hills and had multiple accidents in the days when we didn't wear helmets). One of our neighbors, the Brown family, had two older boys and they had a mini bike and a dirt motorcycle, so that expanded the amount of trails and hills we could explore. I ended up convincing my parents that it would be a good idea if I had a Honda 50 trail bike so that I could ride with my friends. Luckily I was smart enough to wear a helmet, so that I would be protected from my wipeouts and falls. Looking back now, the time on the trails and in the woods around San Carlos would have a strong influence on my love of the outdoors and trail running. Even my Junior High School, Ralston, was situated in the hills of Belmont and our PE time was spent running on the dirt trails behind the school. I can't remember any of the teacher's names, but I give them credit for the fact that I still love to trail run and I'm still doing it more than 50 years later. When I ran cross country in high school, the race course, Crystal Springs, was just down the street from Ralston.

During our time in San Carlos, I had a good friend in fourth grade named Ed Knutson and his parents owned the local bakery. His parents most likely were among the first people I ever met who owned their own business. They rented an apartment close to the bakery and seemed to be working "around the clock", but they also appeared to really love what they were doing. Both my grandparents, and my dad had always worked for "a company." It was good to learn and see first hand the other professions folks had. Ed's dad was not only a talented baker, he was also an artist and during this time the Beatles were really popular and he would draw these great renderings of Paul, Ringo, George and John using a magic marker in the bathroom sink when we had sleep overs - the cool thing is that the white porcelain acted as a white board of sorts that was easy to sketch on and then erase and start over again - and we could add to the drawing before having to brush our teeth, and go to bed.

Chapter 2 - The Heart of the Valley

In the middle of seventh grade, I learned that we would be moving a little farther south to Palo Alto, because my dad's office was moving from San Francisco to Palo Alto on Page Mill Road, right next to Stanford University and the center of what was emerging as Silicon Valley. It was 1972 and I was thirteen.

Looking back it is easy to speculate that if my family had stayed in San Carlos I probably wouldn't have started the companies I did or ended up with an office in the middle of downtown Palo Alto later in 1984. My path would have probably been diverted more towards San Francisco then the Peninsula and I would have missed out on meeting the incredible people who would influence me greatly and make up a good part of this book.

Because of the timing of my dad's move, we ended up switching schools in the middle of the school year, so that the second half of seventh grade would be at Jordan Junior High, about a mile or so from our house. Unlike in Belmont, there would be no school buses to worry about, or giant roller coaster-like streets. Palo Alto was mostly flat and the town had been a pioneer in installing bike lanes on many of the major streets so that I would be able to ride a bike to and from school. Stanford also encouraged bikes as a preferred way to get around campus. The bike culture is alive and well today and encouraged by many local employers, especially Google, as the overall traffic in the Bay Area continues to be a major problem. When I joined Google in June of 2019, I was able to enroll in a 6 month program that allowed me to use a Specialized Turbo E-Bike to commute the 26 miles to and from work each day. It felt great to be able to fly by traffic and reminded me of the freedom of riding around Palo Alto back in the 70s. The big difference was that the amount of cars on the road, especially ones with distracted drivers using their cell phones, had increased significantly and I would need to be on constant alert to make sure that drivers saw me on my bike. I also had been spoiled by being able to take calls in my car going to and from work, which wasn't really an option on the bike. Probably a good thing. On bad traffic days I only would save about 15 minutes each way using my car. My self-powered commutes not only kept a car off the road, but landed me refreshed at work and happy to ride home at night. Then Daylight Savings hit hard and my wife had me reconsidering the safety and sanity of riding as it got darker. Looks like I'll take a break from the bike commute probably until Spring. If it hadn't been for all the time and miles I biked in Palo Alto growing up, I would never have even considered riding again.

Attending high school in Palo Alto in the late 1970s was a lucky break. During this time period there were three high schools in town; Palo Alto, Cubberly and Gunn, since I lived closer to downtown I would be going to Palo Alto High (or "Paly") for the next three years, for 10th, 11th and 12th grade.

What was so special about Paly was the caliber of both the students and the faculty. The close proximity to Stanford also had a heavy influence, as only El Camino Real stood between the Paly campus and Stanford. Many of my classmates had ties to Stanford, as their parents were professors or worked at the university in some capacity.

The time in high school had a heavy influence for a number of reasons and would lay a strong foundation not only for a love of lifetime learning and curiosity, but also a strong tie to Stanford and the resources and people it offered.

I had great teachers, but my favorite by far was Ray Kortan. Ray was the photography teacher, but was also the cross country, soccer and tennis coach. Ray spoke Spanish. He was an avid photographer, but also loved sports and the outdoors. He was known to the students as "Coach Kortan". I spent hours in the photo lab, learning to develop film and print photos, long before digital photography would be introduced. I also ended up on every one of Coach Kortan's teams as I ran cross country, played soccer and tennis all of my years in high school.

What was unique about Coach was that he not only coached us, but also participated with us - he would go on runs through Stanford with the team, stopping by the Tresidder Union Post Office to get his mail and taking us up to the Radar Tower and trails above the University. At one race at Menlo-Atherton High School, the team performed poorly and Coach canceled the return bus back to Paly (about 2.5 miles) and made us run back to school. I could go on and on - but the point is, that Coach was unique and did things his own way and was well respected and liked by his students. My life-long love for running and the outdoors was fueled by Coach Kortan.

During my senior year, my friend Matt Ackerman had decided to buy a 1964 Scout Truck. The only problem was the Scout was located in Sun Valley, Idaho. I'm not sure how we ever got permission, but we convinced our parents that during the week of Spring Break that we would drive with Coach Kortan through the mountains of California to Idaho and pick up the Scout, and then drive back. Matt and I had a good year of driving under our belts. Coach Kortan had two cars, well actually one was a car, the other vehicle was a decommissioned US Mail Truck. We took the red 1970 Opel Kadett Station Wagon. We also would go skiing in Utah and Idaho. Since we had three drivers, we would each take turns and drive straight through to Idaho, pick up the Scout, do some skiing, and then head back via Utah, ski some more and return to California in time to go back to school.

Unfortunately, there had been a drought that winter in Idaho, so there was no snow, so our skiing in Sun Valley was not happening. Ironically, when we left California, we hit a major snow storm going to Lake Tahoe on Highway 80. It was my leg to drive and both Matt and Coach Kortan were asleep. It was dark, snowing, and I'm driving alongside big rigs that would pass and shake the little Opel, but also throw bucket loads of snow on the windshield. I was terrified.

I finally woke up Coach and had him drive, as I wanted us all to at least make it safely out of California.

As dawn broke, we were getting close to Ketchum, Idaho, and would meet the current owner to pick-up the Scout. Matt's parents owned a place in Ketchum and had been spending summers in the Sun Valley area for years and one of their neighbors was selling the Scout. We had breakfast and then the second half of our journey began with Matt and I driving the Scout and Coach driving the Opel.

The Scout had no radio, and very little else on its dashboard. It also was tilted to one side, as there was a bit of a suspension issue that was not disclosed prior to the purchase. We drove it anyway. The one way drive was about 750 miles. Our drive back would be longer, as we were going towards Salt Lake City, so that we could ski.

There was one other quirk the Coach had. He was very frugal (cheap). You may not have noticed, but so far on the trip, we only stopped once to eat (we had packed food and snacks in the car) and we have been sleeping in the car. We would finally stay in a motel in Utah. But first we would almost freeze to death. It was right outside of Salt Lake, it was late and Coach convinced us that getting a motel didn't make sense, and we should just sleep at a rest stop, go skiing in the morning and then check in at the end of the next day. Brilliant. Except, the inside of the Scout was like a giant walk-in freezer, our sleeping bags were thin and better suited for a suburban family room, not below freezing conditions. We woke in the morning and had to scrape ice from inside all of the windows. Coach had the back length of his station wagon well equipped for this type of overnight adventure. He was warm and slept well.

This was 1977, our entire trip was cash based. No credit cards. Simple. I think we called and checked-in with our parents once in Utah, when we had a phone in our room that we could use. We had a paper map. It is amazing what you can do with just a little.

Driving back to California we hit a major snow storm, the snow was coming down so fast that the windshield wipers on the Scout couldn't keep up, and we had to stop and clear the windshield by hand.

We finally made it back to Palo Alto.

One of my classmates in Coach Kortan's Photography class was Dave Shultz. Schultz began wrestling at our junior high school (David Starr Jordan Middle School) and he was coached by Bob Hoskins, one of our shop teachers. Little did I know at the time that Dave would become a seven-time World and Olympic medalist. One clue might have been his habit of always wearing his wrestling singlet under his street clothes. We would often fake wrestle on campus, and he would try to teach me moves. At the time I knew Dave was a good wrestler, but what I didn't realize was that as a senior in high school, he became state champion. That year he also won both his first national and international wrestling titles. As a high school senior he pinned 2-time NCAA champion and NCAA "Outstanding Wrestler" Chuck Yagla at the Great Plains Championships. His brother Mark started competing in sports in gymnastics, winning the Northern California All-Around Gymnastics Championships in his age group. In his junior year he switched to wrestling, and in his senior year won state.

I remember Dave traveling to then - Soviet Georgia to participate in the Tbilisi Tournament. This international tournament is considered to be one of the toughest tournaments in the world. Schultz earned a silver medal and was the highest-placing American at the tournament. Due to the timing of Tbilisi, Schultz was not able to compete in the high school tournaments that he needed to compete in to qualify for the California State Championships, but his coach Ed Hart successfully petitioned the state coaches association to allow him to compete. Wrestling two weight classes above his normal division, Schultz pinned all his opponents in the state championships but the last opponent, whom he defeated 12–1 in the final match. Later that year he won his first national title by winning the U.S. National Open Greco-Roman Championships and won the award for most falls in the least amount of time. Schultz's senior year is considered by many in the wrestling community to be the most successful senior year in U.S. high school wrestling history. To most of us, Dave was simply a good friend, who liked to wrestle and had an unusual amount of trophies on display next to the school office (for those who even knew they were there).

At various times, Schultz also served as an assistant coach at the University of Oklahoma, Stanford University and the University of Wisconsin-Madison. Among many other top U.S. wrestlers, Schultz trained 1996 Olympic Gold Medalist Kurt Angle, who later became a professional wrestler. In the 1990s, he worked as a coach for John du Pont's "Team Foxcatcher", which trained at a complex built on the du Pont family farm in Newton Square, Pennsylvania. In 1996, Schultz was murdered there by John du Pont.

Our 20th high school reunion in 1997 became a tribute to Dave and his legacy. Dave had been training at the Foxcatcher center while preparing for another Olympic bid, as well as coaching the wrestling team. On January 26, 1996, he was shot and killed by du Pont, the owner of the center. Du Pont had exhibited bizarre and threatening behavior for an extended period preceding the murder.

Schultz was 36 at the time of his death. It didn't make sense and at the trial, neither the prosecution nor the defense suggested a motive for the crime. Du Pont was sentenced and died in prison on December 9, 2010. Schultz's father Philip told *The New York Times*, that "the fact that he's officially gone is almost a moot point. I did forgive the man for what he did. I never forgave the act." Later in 2014, the story of the events leading to Dave's death are portrayed in the film Foxcatcher. Having known Dave, it's chilling to watch the film.

After Schultz's murder, 20 former Foxcatcher athletes were left without training or coaching resources six months before the 1996 Olympic Games. Schultz's widow founded the Dave Schultz Wrestling Club in March 1996 to sponsor the stranded wrestlers through the Olympics. The Club succeeded beyond the initial goal. It continued to train athletes in both men's and women's wrestling until it closed in 2005.

What was so special about growing up in Palo Alto at this time was that people like Dave had the support of dedicated coaches and mentors that allowed them to thrive and accomplish world class achievements. To a certain degree, this seemed pretty normal in our high school so close to Stanford.

The parents of many of my classmates created a culture of entrepreneurship as well. For example, the father of my classmate Amy, was a doctor, but what I didn't know until later was that he was a pioneering heart transplant surgeon. Dr. Norman Shumway led a Stanford team that performed the first human heart transplant in the United States on Jan. 6, 1968. He also pioneered other open heart surgical procedures. The 1968 heart transplant patient, 54-year-old steelworker Mike Kasperak, lived just 14 days and many hospitals gave up on heart transplants because of the high mortality rate. But Shumway continued the operations.

"Many people gave it up when they thought it was too difficult, but Dr. Shumway had the persistence and vision that it could work," said Dr. Bruce Reitz, Stanford professor of cardiothoracic surgery. "His determination to make heart transplantation work was absolutely crucial." Nearly 60,000 Americans have had heart transplants over the years, including 1,240 at Stanford.

Shumway, speaking at a 2003 gathering of transplant patients to help celebrate his 80th birthday, said it was "gratifying to see the changes that have made this (heart transplant) an almost ordinary experience."

Another parent who stood out was Peter Young's dad, John. Being clueless high school students, none of us knew what Peter's dad did for a living. When we would visit his house, his mom, brother and sister would be around, but we never seemed to see his dad, John. One day there was a group of us together and someone asked Peter, where does your dad work? Peter answered simply: "HP in Palo Alto" and we went on with our conversations. What Peter failed to mention was that his dad joined Hewlett-Packard in 1958, rising to the post of vice president in 1968. He was elected executive vice president and a director in 1974. Young succeeded William Hewlett as president of Hewlett-Packard in 1977, receiving the titles of chief operating officer in 1977 and chief executive officer in 1978.

Following the founders of a company with the culture of HP is no easy task and John Young did an exceptional job. The incredible culture that Bill & Dave built was something that John Young had been a part of, so it was natural for an insider to take over the CEO role, having experienced so much first hand. The HP succession of leadership reminded me of the subsequent basketball coaches at UCLA that followed John Wooden. Who would want to take over and be compared to Wooden? When Coach Wooden retired in 1975, Gene Bartow took over and only lasted until 1977 when I became a freshman. By the time I graduated, four years later in 1981, we had gone through three more coaches. Gary Cunningham, 1977-1979. Larry Brown, 1979-1981 and Larry Farmer, 1981-1984.

Peter and I would later work together for a short time at Macromedia in San Francisco. He had gone to UC Santa Barbara and studied Computer Science and worked as a software developer at Apple on the original Lisa computer team. It was Peter who suggested the restaurant that I took my wife, Jill, on our first date in Saratoga. Since Peter lived in Cupertino, and I was still in Palo Alto, I had called him for a recommendation for something in the South Bay. Jill and I celebrated our 37th wedding anniversary in February 2022. Thanks, Peter!.

The Palo Alto/Stanford pattern would be repeated over and over again. The people and connections I made in this world would greatly influence my future and what I worked on in the years to come. There is something uniquely special about the Bay Area and the combination of people, environment, curiosity for learning and openness to new ideas was highly motivational to anyone contemplating starting something new.

My father-in-law, Jim Palmquist, was another example of an entrepreneur in the early days of Silicon Valley. He started Intercity Office Machines in San Jose and later moved the business to Santa Clara, just as companies such as Intel were getting their start. Intel was an early customer of Intercity, buying typewriters and adding machines to help their growing business.

One of the most important lessons I learned is that location can really matter and there's a reason that so many companies from Hewlett-Packard to Google were started in the Bay Area. This trend is in the process of changing, and there are always exceptions, but if you want to improve your odds, there is definitely an advantage to the location you choose.

As I write this, in late June, 2020, Facebook has just announced that most employees will work remotely through the end of the year, though it expects its offices will open for a small number of employees starting in July. Google has initiated a similar policy for the team I currently work on.

Facebook will become far more friendly to remote work, founder and CEO Mark Zuckerberg announced recently in a livestream to employees that was shared publicly. "We're going to be the most forward-leaning company on remote work at our scale," Zuckerberg said. "I think that it's quite possible that over the next five to 10 years, about 50 percent of our people could be working remotely."

Currently, more than 50 percent of Facebook employees now work from home due to the pandemic that started in early March 2020. The company has told workers they'll be free to work remotely through the end of 2020. But even after the COVID-19 threat subsides, Facebook will be more accepting of remote workers than it was before the pandemic.

The jury is out on how this will ultimately work out and what it will do in the long term to team dynamics and productivity. Personally, I think there needs to be a balance between virtual and remote work and actually being present.

From my experience, the chance meetings and serendipity that happens at lunch or happy hour or informal encounters pays huge benefits. A video meeting can't compete.

To emphasize this point, I remember the stories about the intense planning for the interior design of the space at Pixar headquarters in Emeryville, California. The story behind Pixar's headquarters starts in 1999 with Steve Jobs. As Pixar's CEO, Jobs brought in Bohlin Cywinski Jackson – known for designing Bill Gates' Washington residential compound – to discuss his vision for the campus, which was planned to hold up to 1000 employees.

According to Jobs' biography, the headquarters was to be a place that "promoted encounters and unplanned collaborations." Given collaboration was one of the major topics in office design, and that the late 90's were filled with cubicle farms, his ideas were clearly ahead of the curve.

Jobs also strived for a campus that stood the test of time. Tom Carlisle, Pixar's facilities director adds that, "He didn't want a standard office-park building—one with corrugated-metal siding or ribbon windows. The building had to look good 100 years from now. That was his main criterion." Pixar's campus design originally separated different employee disciplines into different buildings – one for computer scientists, another for animators, and a third building for everybody else. But because Jobs was fanatical about these unplanned collaborations, he envisioned a campus where these encounters could take place, and his design included a great atrium space that acts as a central hub for the campus.

The biography adds that Jobs believed that, "If a building doesn't encourage collaboration, you'll lose a lot of innovation and the magic that's sparked by serendipity. So we designed the building to make people get out of their offices and mingle in the central atrium with people they might not otherwise see."

The atrium houses a reception, employee mailboxes, cafe, foosball, fitness center, two 40-seat viewing rooms, and a large theater – and was planned by Jobs to house the campus' only restrooms. The idea was that people who naturally isolate themselves would be forced to have great conversations, even if that took place while washing their hands. Today, they do have more than one restroom, of course. But it was the idea behind it that was important.

And did it work? "Steve's theory worked from day one," said John Lasseter, Pixar's chief creative officer "...I've never seen a building that promoted collaboration and creativity as well as this one."

This same approach is everywhere at Google and I'm always amazed and surprised at the time and effort that goes into the interiors of the various offices that I've visited. Most companies just refuse to take the extra time, thought and money to design spaces that encourage collaboration and creativity.

This discipline is not limited to tech. At a small gathering in San Francisco that I attended a few years ago, I listened to Joe Lacob, a venture capitalist turned majority owner of the Golden State Warriors explain that one of the first things he did when he took over the Warriors was to change the office space and get rid of all the private offices. The accounting team was up in arms and said "they needed the private space to make sure that no one saw the financials" Joe countered that "the numbers are so bad, nobody cares".

He came to realize that most NBA teams separate their business operations from the players and coaches and they seldom collaborate or interact. To make matters worse, the business folks were isolated in their work space. Windows were added, walls were torn down and weekly meetings between the business team and the coaching staff were a regular event. There were many other things that Lacob and his organization did, but this one is rarely mentioned when talking about what helped the Warriors win championships in the 2014-15, 2016-17, and 2017-18 NBA seasons.

Chapter 3 - Coast to Coast

In the Summer of 1977, I graduated from Paly and had decided to attend UCLA in the Fall. Earlier in the year my dad had taken a new job at Digital Equipment Corp in Nashua, New Hampshire, and had been renting a house in the small town of Amherst, New Hampshire, while my mom, sister and I stayed in Palo Alto to finish out the school year.

In the first week that my dad arrived in New England from Northern California he witnessed one of the worst snow storms from a dark, dingy motel room off Route 3 in Nashua, NH. It was an incredible contrast to sunny California and he was wondering if he had made a wise decision to switch coasts and leave his family.

Personally, I was lucky, because I felt like I had the best of both coasts. I could experience the incredible contrast between rural New England, the San Francisco Bay Area and Los Angeles during the next couple of years, as I traveled back and forth from the West to the East Coast. Besides what I was learning at UCLA, because of my dad's work at Digital, I was getting an early education on the impact that computers were going to make throughout the next several decades.

UCLA was an incredible place to go to college. Originally, I had hoped to go to Brown University in Providence, Rhode Island and also be able to take classes at neighboring Rhode Island School of Design (RISD). Since my parents were now going to be in New Hampshire, I figured it made sense to go to a college that was closer. A couple of things interfered with my plans. First, I did a quick tour at the end of my senior year in high school, and we got lost in a "white out" snow storm trying to find Middlebury College in Vermont. Los Angeles was looking better and better. My application to Brown was also rejected.

I enrolled at UCLA in the Fall of 1977, I was just seventeen. I was going to study Design in the Fine Arts College. Design was a broad category and at the time the school was struggling with a tension between teaching pure theory or preparing students with practical skills that could be used in the workplace. Ideally it would be good to get a bit of both, but the thinking at the time was to focus on the theory, skills be damned. Luckily I decided to work on campus and although I started with one job, I ended up with two jobs that both helped me to gain important skills and real-life experience.

The first job was working for ASUCLA (Associated Students of University of California Los Angeles) in the student store on campus. The store was the second largest college bookstore in the US, second only to Harvard. I was hired by Ruth Ann Hartman, who had spent most of her career as the advertising and marketing manager for the store. The job involved working with all of the individual departments such as books, electronics, clothing, etc. to market their products. The primary mechanism used was creating newspaper advertising for the Daily Bruin, the UCLA campus paper. We also did all of the in-store signage and promotional materials. Perhaps the biggest project of all was the yearly catalog with all of the UCLA merchandise - the Bearwear Catalog that was mailed out to alumni, faculty and staff each Fall.

Working at ASUCLA gave me a very good understanding of what it was like to work with different "clients", to come up with creative ideas and to meet daily deadlines. What I was learning would serve me well later when I started my own design firm in Palo Alto. I also got my first taste of being close to the customer, as a student myself, I was the intended customer in most cases.

The newspaper at the time was in the middle of pioneering a new "digital" typesetting system that we had access to. The good news was that we were on the bleeding edge of technology for producing our daily ad materials that would be published the next day. The bad news was the system often crashed and didn't work correctly and meant that you would have to try something multiple times to get it right. Learning how to manage the transition from working traditionally—using manual tools to physically "paste-up" art boards that would be turned into finished ads—to preparing all of the materials and getting a proof on a computer all at once was the future, and we were able to use the resources of the university to get a glimpse of what would become the norm in the years to come.

At the same time, I ended up taking another part time campus job at the Biomedical Library with the responsibility to prepare monthly exhibits at the entrance of the library that highlighted the collection and various topics that the staff considered important. The real reason I took the job, though, was that I was given access to my own private studio full of art supplies in the private stacks (the area that stored rare books). The freedom and responsibility the library gave me as a student was a big motivator to wanting to work independently after graduation.

For example, right next to my work space was a copy of **The Birds of America**, a book by naturalist and painter John James Audubon, containing illustrations of a wide variety of birds of the United States. It was first published as a series in sections between 1827 and 1838, in Edinburgh and London. The book was amazing and contained 435 hand-coloured, life-size prints, made from engraved plates.

I couldn't believe that I was getting paid to work in the library. In addition to such rare books there were surgical instruments from the early 1900s, crazy saws and instruments in old wooden boxes. The studio also served as a place for me to do my design projects for school. Not only was it quiet, but it was immense, and allowed me plenty of room to spread out and work. Living space was tight on campus and I shared my room with two other guys, so having the space in the library was a real advantage and helped me do well in school.

The other positive was that I was getting exposed to an entirely different aspect of the UCLA campus - the medical and scientific side vs. the fine arts side where the majority of my classes were. Dickson Art Center and the Biomedical Library were completely different and on either end of the vast campus. Being exposed to such opposite disciplines and thinking was a very important experience.

I remember many years later talking with Don Knuth, a computer scientist and professor emeritus at Stanford. He and his wife Jill attended the same church we did in Menlo Park, Bethany Lutheran. Don told me that he had encouraged his computer science students to take design classes and for design students to try computer science. He created the TeX computer typesetting system, and the Computer Modern family of typefaces. In 1974 he received the ACM Turing Award, informally considered the Nobel Prize of computer science. The other thing I remember about Don was that he told me he was retiring from using email. He wanted to focus on finishing his book. It was 1990.

He issued a public statement on his faculty page that read:

I have been a happy man ever since January 1, 1990, when I no longer had an email address. I'd used email since about 1975, and it seems to me that 15 years of email is plenty for one lifetime.

Email is a wonderful thing for people whose role in life is to be on top of things. But not for me; my role is to be on the bottom of things. What I do takes long hours of studying and uninterruptible concentration. I try to learn certain areas of computer science exhaustively; then I try to digest that knowledge into a form that is accessible to people who don't have time for such study.

On the other hand, I need to communicate with thousands of people all over the world as I write my books. I also want to be responsive to the people who read those books and have questions or comments. My goal is to do this communication efficiently, in batch mode --- like, one day every six months. So if you want to write to me about any topic, please use good ol' snail mail and send a letter to the following address:

Prof. Donald E. Knuth

Computer Science Department
Gates Building 4B
Stanford University
Stanford, CA 94305-9045 USA.

    Don also had another piece of wisdom. He said that every Sunday after the church service he goes out of his way to meet someone new. Our natural tendency is to gravitate to our friends, but by doing so we miss out on a perfect opportunity to not only meet someone new, but also to learn new things. Don would always go out of his way to learn and be curious.

    My time at UCLA was special and I couldn't have asked for a better place to learn. As a freshman, I ended up moving out of my dorm room in Rieber Hall to 613 Gayley, the Phi Kappa Psi fraternity house. Unlike many of the other houses on campus and the heavy stereotypes that both fraternities and sororities carry, Phi Psi seemed different. We had a diverse group of guys, with different backgrounds and interests. The one thing in common was that the majority of the house was from Southern California, specifically West LA and Orange County. There were a few of us from Northern California, but we were definitely the exception. Living in a house for almost 4 years with such a wide variety of people was eye opening. Looking back, I probably learned more from my fraternity brothers than any of the professors I ever had. One of those people was Doug Cosman, or as we called him "Cosmo". Cosmo was from New York, and loved rock and roll and had the 70's long hair to prove it. As a guitarist, I remember him playing for the Andrea True Connection, the band that had a hit song in 1976, "More, More, More" He and I would often do our laundry on the weekends at a West LA laundromat, and then go to the music store next door and check out all the guitars. But Doug was realistic about making it as a rock and roll star. He ended up earning a Bachelor's Degree in Computer Science at the University of Colorado in Boulder. He got married, had kids and founded a company in Boulder, called YieldEx. I learned recently that he had passed away in 2016 of pancreatic cancer.

Being exposed to such a wide variety of amazing people during college reminded me of the similar experiences back in Palo Alto. The other unique element at UCLA was Hollywood. Many of my classmates had parents in show business. Jim Rosen's father, Arnie, was a writer and producer who had won five Emmys for his television work on shows like The Carol Burnett Show. But in the fraternity television room, we were focused on "Get Smart" reruns and whether the episode was an "Arnie". I often wondered what it was like to go to work and come up with the ideas and writing for an episode of "Get Smart" and how much fun it had to be? How did they come up with the "shoe phone" and the "cone of silence"? I wish I would have taken the time to ask Jim's dad.

In 1979, Tim Moore, another fraternity brother, had just graduated and was looking for something to do. I'm not sure how he got connected, but there was a movie being produced called "1941" that needed extras and Tim convinced a number of us to sign-up. The premise of the movie was that after Japan's attack on Pearl Harbor, residents of California descend into a wild panic, afraid that they might be the next target. Among them are Wild Bill Kelso (John Belushi), a crazed National Guard pilot; Sgt. Frank Tree (Dan Aykroyd), a patriotic, straight-laced tank crew commander. This was Steven Spielberg's attempt at screwball comedy, and it was pretty lame. The best part for us was that we were paid and fed for 3 nights of filming. The downside was that we had to get military haircuts to look the part at a time when long hair was the norm.

Perhaps the funniest part of the experience was that as extras we were supposed to park at the Hollywood Bowl and take a bus into the studio. On the second night, someone decided that we would just drive directly to the studio in our sailor costumes. When we arrived at the security gate, we waved, saying we were in 1941 and to our amazement, we were waved through and parked right on the set. The sad part was that there were thousands of extras and many thought that this would be their "break" into show business. The odds were not in their favor. Having

Dan Aykroyd and John Belushi on the set was memorable, but on the third night, a comedian named Robin Williams stopped by to watch the filming and hang out with his friends. Only in LA could something like this happen to a kid in college.

Tim Moore went on to become a successful producer and production manager, and is still going strong today. If you look closely at the credits for any of Clint Eastwood's recent movies, Tim is the Executive Producer. And to think he got started by convincing a bunch of college guys to cut their hair and wear sailor suits.

Another one of our fraternity brothers, John Shepherd, was an actor and producer who has starred in film and on television. He is best known for his role in the 1985 horror film "Friday the 13th". What's ironic about that role is that he had to wear a mask. I remember convincing Jill, who I had just married, that she had to go see this movie because my friend, John, was in it. She was not a horror film fan, but went along with me! Perhaps the best story involving John was an audition that he didn't get called back for. Not one to give up, John went back the next day using a different name and appearance. The casting person stopped the audition midstream, "wait, is that John?" and had to laugh at John's determination. He still didn't get the part. He also got really close to a part for a sitcom called "Cheers" - he auditioned for the part of bartender Woody Boyd. A guy named "Woody Harrelson" beat him out for the part. John never gave up on his passion and still works in the entertainment industry today.

As graduation approached, I wasn't sure what I wanted to do once I finished UCLA. I really liked Los Angeles and all it had to offer at the time. Since my parents were no longer in Northern California, I really didn't have much of a reason to settle back in the Bay Area. I graduated in the Summer of 1981 and moved to Brentwood with one of my fraternity brothers, Brad Livingston, who was a year older and had been working in the advertising industry in Downtown LA. As I started to look for jobs, I ended up at CBS's Television City, a studio complex located in the Fairfax District of Los Angeles. Since its inauguration in 1952, numerous TV shows have been broadcast live or taped at Television City. I was hired to work in the advertising department which sounded glamorous, but in reality, was far from it, as I spent the majority of my time in a dark room, preparing artwork for TV Guide Ads. About a month into the job, I received a call from ASUCLA, the bookstore where I had worked during college. My old boss, Ruth Ann, had quit unexpectedly and they were looking for a replacement and heard that I worked at CBS in advertising. No one bothered to ask what I did at CBS, and I was hired to manage the advertising department for the Students' Store. No interview, no resume. I now had a real job, with employees.

I would be responsible for all the daily advertising and promotion for the various store departments, as well as the direct mail catalogs, store signage and displays and to top it off, preparation for the 1984 Summer Olympics that were coming to Los Angeles, with UCLA as one of the venues. Talk about a learning experience. My peers were decades older and had so much more experience than I did - what I did have going for me was that I was much closer to the target audience, as I had just graduated and had a good sense of what students were looking for. Since I didn't know any better, I was also willing to take incredible risks, as I had little to lose. There were two examples that really stand out and for which I'm lucky I didn't get fired for.

The first crazy idea I had was to do an ad for the book department with the headline "We're Bullish on Books" I wanted to play on the popular commercials that the investment firm Merrill Lynch was running in 1981. I learned from my roommate Brad, that the bulls that Merrill Lynch used for their 30-second spot television commercials were located in Los Angeles and he had the contact information. What I didn't know until later is that they would use two bulls. Why two bulls when only one appears in the commercials? "Yes, we only show a single bull, but you can't do anything with only one," said Merrill Lynch's vice president for marketing, James Walsh. "A bull gets very tense by himself.

He has to have a buddy along. They're not the brightest animals in the world."

Be that as it may, in one of the new commercials, the filmed bull walks through a field of haystacks and manages to discover a needle in a haystack. This is a metaphor for Merrill Lynch's research facilities and investment-spotting expertise. In the other commercial, the bull walks through a greenhouse to show metaphorically that, as Merrill Lynch puts it, the company "can nurture all your investment needs."

So I put together a purchase order for "one bull" to be photographed walking through the Student Store's Book Department. What could possibly go wrong? Not much as it turned out. The bull behaved and we were able to take photos in the store surrounded by all the textbooks. (this was before Photoshop - so doing the ad digitally was not an option) The ad campaign was a success and we ended up getting some extra publicity in the school paper, *The Daily Bruin*. We probably missed out on a lot of additional PR, but I hadn't really thought about that, I was just trying to make sure I didn't destroy the store and lose my job. The only downside was one of the store employees refused to come into work that day, since he was deathly afraid of bulls.

The other big risk involved one of my fraternity brothers, Tony, who was still in school. His brother was a student at USC and I wanted to do a campaign for the upcoming crosstown rivalry USC vs. UCLA football game. I had the idea to dress USC's mascot "Tommy Trojan" in UCLA gear, including placing one of our store shopping bags in Tommy's hand and using it in a newspaper ad with the headline: "I'd rather switch than fight" So Tony and I drove over to USC very early in the morning, right before sunrise, loaded up with UCLA clothing with directions on how to find "Tommy" What we didn't plan for was how high off the ground the actual statue was. We quickly climbed up and dressed the statue, took photos and returned to Westwood. I'm curious who discovered "UCLA Tommy" first on the SC campus the next morning. In recent times, the statue is heavily guarded and covered to avoid damage. I'm not sure if our little prank had anything to do with the current security but I'm sure glad no one caught us.

Besides working on daily advertising, I also had the responsibility for two direct mail catalogs that were sent out to students and alumni and anyone else interested in UCLA merchandise. During this time we discovered that we had developed a strong brand and passionate following in Japan. Tour buses would show up at the store and customers would literally buy our "Bearwear" by the bus load. We even printed signage in Japanese to help guide people to the merchandise. My manager at the time had international licensing experience and we went a step further and licensed the "UCLA" brand to Descente Ltd., a Japanese sports clothing and accessories company so they could begin selling merchandise directly in Japan. This was a big win for our group, especially since the Associated Students of UCLA was a non-profit organization.

While working on the catalogs I met Jim Frew. In 1955, Frew moved to Los Angeles to pursue a commercial art career. While in California, he worked for various department stores and for the Carson-Roberts Advertising Agency, which held the Mattel toy company account. During his career with Carson-Roberts, which is now Ogilvy & Mather, Frew worked on some national commercials and told me about an experience with the founders of Baskin-Robbins, the Ice Cream Company. Burt Baskin and Irv Robbins had wanted the agency to produce a newspaper ad for their new firm. Jim suggested that the money would be much better spent by designing a logo for their store instead. A national brand was born that is still with us today. I never forgot this lesson from Jim and his subtle way of saying "no" to a client, but offering a much better alternative. It is so easy to go along and give the customer what they ask for, but often it isn't the best solution.

He then left the ad agency and worked independently in Los Angeles. This is when we met and began working together. For the Bearwear Catalog, we used a UCLA student by the name of Heather Locklear, as one of the models on the cover. There was really no formal process to find models. Some of the managers in the store would suggest people or volunteer their kids. I would ask students in the store or on campus if they would be interested in modeling, and if they said "yes" I would tell them the time and location for the job. Most people said "yes".

Frew, semi-retired in 1985 and moved back to Tulsa, where he continued to work as a layout artist for Neiman Marcus catalogs. He began painting after fully retiring. His work has been exhibited in public galleries, one-man shows and private collections. He passed away in 2006 in his hometown of Tulsa. Jim was a true mentor and I'm extremely lucky to have had the opportunity to work and learn from him.

One last thing about Jim. He loved food and wine. One night he invited me to dinner and I brought wine. He suggested we "let it breathe" before drinking it. I had no idea what he was talking about and had to ask. It was another good life lesson for a kid just out of college!

5

Chapter 4 - Return to the Valley

I was very happy working at UCLA. Then one day I received a call out of the blue about the opportunity to work for a start-up software company in Northern California called Softlink. The IBM PC was the leading personal computer and the Apple II was also becoming popular, especially in the Valley. Softlink was a publisher of software, so they didn't actually write code, but worked with programmers to publish and distribute their programs. Software packaging was a big deal in 1983 when I took the job to be Director of Marketing, because it was what buyers saw on the shelf of the computer retailer and helped explain what the software could do. Advertising was also important to drive people to the stores and motivate them to ask for specific products by name. Business software for personal computers during this time was very expensive and hard to use. Softlink was promoting a "try before you buy" concept that allowed you to buy and use the software inexpensively and then upgrade to the full version by getting a code to "unlock" for unlimited usage. It was a great idea, way ahead of its time, but actual sales were slow. The company also struggled to get publishing rights to the best software. Finally, they faced the challenge of getting "shelf space" from the major computer retailers that sold the majority of software. What I didn't realize at the time was that I was learning incredible lessons about software publishing and distribution and what marketing tactics worked in this emerging category. It was also my first introduction to the world of venture-backed start-ups and how they worked. I also met some interesting pioneers like Norman Tu, who we used to copy disks for our products. Today, Norman Tu is Chairman and CEO of DCL Logistics, 38 years ago he began to notice a shift in the industry along with the personal computing boom. In 1982, he worked for Hewlett-Packard, but was eager to pave his own way in the industry. "Some of my colleagues were leaving HP to start their own businesses in the industry. A friend came to me and told me he was copying disks for his software business," Tu said. "He said he didn't enjoy it and wanted to hire me to do it."

Norman took the leap, quit his job at Hewlett-Packard, and began DisCopyLabs. Without the budget for brochures and marketing materials, he chose a name that would need no further explanation. The DisCopyLabs name was designed to immediately communicate copying software to a disc. Within the first 10 years, the business grew exponentially, and in 1992 alone the business had copied 50 million floppy discs.

"There was a need in the marketplace and I provided the service," Norman says. Even though the need for copying disks has gone away, the clients still flock to Norman's business.

What's special about Norman, is that he has been able to adapt his business to continue to add value for his customers almost 40 years since it was founded. DCL Logistics is still going strong today and he is a great example of an entrepreneur who knows how to continue to reinvent their business.

Unfortunately, Softlink's life as a business was short lived and we were short on cash and it looked like my job was in jeopardy. Our office on Scott Blvd. in Santa Clara was spacious and first class. I remember our landlord, John Arrillaga, walking though and quickly showing how we could cut our space in half by adding a wall. I had met John before when I was in high school because he was a close neighbor of my friend Bill Shott. In the 1960s, Arrillaga and business partner Richard Peery bought California farmland and converted it into office space. They became two of Silicon Valley's biggest commercial landlords with more than 12,000,000 square feet. The personal visit by John meant that we were in trouble as a company. It was time to figure out a new job. In my role as the Director of Marketing I had managed a local ad agency that was located in downtown Mountain View and was looking to hire more people as their business was expanding.

One of their clients was a local computer retailer that was selling computers by a new company called "Apple". They offered me a job. It was 1983, and in the past year an impressive number of companies started up in Silicon Valley, a fact that began to alter the relative proportion between hardware and software.

Autodesk was founded in 1981 in Mill Valley in the North Bay. Symantec was founded in March 1982 in Sunnyvale to pursue artificial intelligence-based research, notably in natural-language processing. Symantec went on to specialize in development tools for software engineers, i.e. software to help build other software. Borland was founded in 1983 in Scotts Valley (between San Jose and Santa Cruz) by three Danish developers (Niels Jensen, Ole Henriksen, and Mogens Glad) and Philippe Kahn, a Frenchman who had cut his teeth on the Micral project as a programmer. The Computer History Museum considers the Micral one of the earliest commercial, non-kit personal computers. Borland didn't target the growing needs of the end user but of the software developer. My wife, Jill, would work at Borland for a short period in 1985. Because of her job in Scotts Valley, we almost moved from Palo Alto to Santa Cruz, because the commute on Highway 17 could be treacherous, as the road winds through the Santa Cruz Mountains towards the sea.

John Warnock and Charles Geschke left Xerox PARC, where they had worked on the page-description language InterPress for Xerox's laser printer, to develop a simpler language, PostScript, and they founded Adobe in december 1982 in Mountain View to commercialize it. PostScript was the first building block for desktop publishing, which still needed a viable computer platform and a suitable software environment (both unsuccessfully pioneered by Xerox's Star). Unlike most startups, Adobe was profitable from its first year.

Intuit, founded in 1983 by Scott Cook and Tom Proulx in Palo Alto, offered Quicken, a personal finance management tool for the Apple II. Designed by Proulx, it was a personal finance management tool running on the IBM PC and the Apple II.

Once I started to work at the ad agency I noticed the need of all these new software companies for marketing and advertising help, especially product packaging for their "shrink-wrapped" software that needed to not only get shelf space, but get the attention of customers and sell through retail. The agency was much more focused on newspaper advertising and wasn't interested in pursuing the package design angle that I was passionate about. I decided to start my own company out of my apartment in downtown Palo Alto.

Thinking back to the lesson I learned from Norman Tu, on company naming, I kept it simple, and "Rollinson Design" was founded in 1994. As luck would have it, I was also introduced to Heidi Roizen, who would become my first client and best salesperson. I recently visited Heidi, 35 years later and we laughed and reminisced at her office on Sand Hill Road in Menlo Park. It was strange to be back at a venture capital office without pitching a new company or trying to raise money. I actually got lost and wandered around the wrong hallway, in the wrong building before finding Heidi's office. We talked about our families and caught up. Back when we met, Heidi had recently graduated from Stanford Business School and was co-founder and CEO of T/Maker Company, which made software for CP/M and MS-DOS computers, and later for the Apple Macintosh. Her brother, Peter Roizen was the other co-founder; he had graduated from the University of California, Berkeley, and had written the original software named "Table Maker" that had launched the company. From 1987 until 1994, Roizen also served on the board of directors of the Software Publishers Association and was its president from 1988 to 1990.

Having T/Maker as my first client not only proved to be extremely important to growing the business, but also would play an important role in some of my later ventures that went beyond design. In real estate the old saying is that "location, location, location" is a key to success. In technology, I learned early on, how important "timing, timing, timing" was as well. When timing and location are in sync with the right people, amazing things can happen.

The time was 1984 and after doing some initial design work for Heidi and her team, a new opportunity surfaced. The opportunity was to do the product development, marketing and design work for a new software product for the Macintosh that T/Maker was going to not only produce but also publish. Folks at Apple had reached out to Heidi to create a line of clip art for the Macintosh that showed off the amazing graphic capabilities. Together we created "ClickArt", the fifth software title available for the Mac. As a designer, I was able to see the potential of the Mac right away and was lucky enough to get to use pre-release machines to start to create some of the initial art. We ended up hiring a small group of traditional artists to do the original work. One of the artists, Greg Clarke, had been a friend and classmate from UCLA, and he actually moved up to Palo Alto for the length of the project and stayed downtown in the Cardinal Hotel with a Mac and began drawing with a mouse. Greg also illustrated the cover for this book!

One of the other artists was an architect. No one had ever used a computer to draw with before and all were very skeptical to begin with about this new medium. Since there were no external hard drives yet, storing and creating images required you to keep inserting multiple floppy disks into the one drive, over and over again. When we had finally assembled enough of a portfolio of images, we released the software and it sold well. One of the mistakes I initially made with the packaging was that I wanted us to use small plastic boxes with a label wrap. Unfortunately, all of the software was being sold in retail computer locations and shelf space was important and large boxes got more attention and tended to sell through better. We ended up changing the packaging to a more traditional approach.

I quickly outgrew my apartment and leased an office in downtown Palo Alto on Hamilton Ave. My landlord was a landscape architect, Ken Arutunian, Co-founder of Arutunian Kinney & Associates (AKA), Ken worked as a landscape architect in the Bay Area for more than forty years. With his sister, Carol Arutunian, he also established the first European-style cafe in Palo Alto, Café Verona. My office was in the rear of the cafe and we later expanded to the second floor with a view looking down on the cafe below.

Today the building is a trendy spot for high-end Mexican fare with a popular bar scene thanks to their margarita selection. The restaurant was opened in 2009 by Rob Fischer, who also owns the Palo Alto Creamery, right down the street.

Back in 1984, the cafe had a manager named Fred, and he was a stickler about allowing anyone to bring outside food into the cafe. One customer loved the coffee in the cafe, but also liked the bagels served a couple doors down the street. This particular customer would often hide out with his bagel and coffee and do everything he could to not get noticed by Fred. On many occasions I would look down from my desk and watch this "cat and mouse" game play out between Fred and the customer. The customer was Steve Jobs. Soon he would be fired from Apple and start NeXT. Jobs didn't just have his morning bagel and coffee in the cafe. He would also do business and I witnessed an intense conversation one afternoon in 1986 that was the beginning of Steve buying Pixar. Jobs acquired the computer graphics division of Lucasfilm, Ltd. and renamed it Pixar Animation Studios. He remained CEO and majority shareholder at 50.1% until its acquisition by The Walt Disney Company on May 5, 2006.

I recently learned of another interesting conversation that took place at Café Verona in 1998. My friend and former colleague, Delly Tamer, grabbed his coffee and headed to a small table where Reed Hastings, his boss at the time, was waiting. Reed had something important on his mind. "Delly, Marc and I are considering a BIG strategy change. I want to get your take." Reed and Marc Randolph had co-founded Netflix the year before. Delly was running business development and helping with Marketing. "We are considering eliminating DVD sales to focus on rentals and streaming. I'd like your opinion before I make a final decision". Immediately, he could tell I was stunned. "Wait, aren't DVD sales about 95% of our revenues?" Ever so precise, Reed replied "97%". My jaw dropped. "And you want to stop that? Why?" Reed launched into his argument. The site was too complex, customers were having trouble navigating between sales and rentals, and margins were eroding at a fast clip.

Delly's mind was spinning. He thought they had lost their minds, but before he gave his opinion, he asked him a question. "Reed, my opinion depends on one thing. You have already invested $2 Million of your own money in Netflix and you own 70% of it. Do you intend to pour more of your own money or do you plan to raise funds from venture capitalists?"

It was his turn to pause and I could tell my question had an impact, but his answer was clear. "Delly, I want to raise money from VC's". It was my turn to launch into a passionate counter-argument and detail why this was a terrible idea.

"We both know that the VC's have not been very, shall we say, receptive to us. They want to see revenue growth and DVD sales will contribute heavily to our top line." A partner at a top 5 venture capital firm had dismissed Netflix, proclaiming he did not invest in companies destined to remain small.

Reed countered: "If Amazon gets into the game, they'll destroy us. Margins will quickly go to zero." I did not relent. "Amazon is a giant with 600 employees, but they have too many fish to fry." I piled on another argument about customer satisfaction, where I raised the specter of angry customers at the lack of choice. I added: "Don't we want to be the one-stop shop for all things flix"?

We debated back and forth, but eventually, Reed made up his mind. He said "Delly, I hear you, but I am not convinced, so I am going to go with the decision to eliminate DVD sales". Immediately, I took out a paper pad from my backpack, set it on the table, and replied: "OK, Reed. How do we execute?"

It was his turn to be taken aback. He looked at me with his intense eyes and said:

"Wait, just like that? Are you ready to go along with this decision? You were so passionate about why we should not do that". I smiled. "Reed, you are the co-CEO. I greatly appreciate you giving me an opportunity to voice my opinion, but once you make the final call, my job is to follow it to the letter. We all need to move in the same direction."

Netflix's ability to execute came down to Reed and Marc communicating their decision and tracking its implementation. While they eradicated DVD sales in a few weeks, streaming ended up taking eight years.

Reed's initial goal was for us to launch streaming in 2002, but it wasn't until late 2006 that streaming debuted. Had he ever given in to the enormous pressure from Wall Street to drop it, Netflix would be an insignificant company today.

In Delly's opinion, Reed Hastings's single biggest accomplishment at Netflix in the past 22 years was his multi-year perseverance at launching streaming against all odds without ever wavering. It was the best business decision he ever made. Back in those days, big decisions were debated face-to-face, just like Reed and Delly did in the cafe.

As my office on Hamilton Avenue grew, there was also an incredible amount of new software being created. T/Maker was growing and expanding and Heidi's connections to Stanford helped attract talent to the company. Royal Farros and Robert Simon had both graduated from Stanford and were working at T/Maker. It was also a family affair, besides Heidi's brother writing software, her mom Gisel worked shipping out software. Often Gisel would try to tell Heidi how to "run" the company. I wish I had paid closer attention to the daily dialog between mother and daughter.

What I did pay attention to was how Heidi and her team were building a successful software company and I was along for the ride. Hanging out at the T/Maker offices was becoming part of my routine and it seemed like each time I visited a new project would appear. I was also starting to get referral business from Heidi's vast network of people starting software companies.

The next project was to design the packaging for another Mac software product. T/Maker was my client, but I'd have to also get design approval from the person that owned the rights to the software. The program was WriteNow, originally written for Apple Computer, Inc. by John Anderson and Bill Tschumy in Seattle, separate from the Macintosh computer and MacWrite word processor development teams. Steve Jobs was concerned that those programming MacWrite were not going to be ready for the 1984 release date of the Macintosh; he therefore commissioned a team of programmers to work independently on a similar project, which eventually became WriteNow. Members of the WriteNow team knew about MacWrite, but members of the MacWrite team did not know about WriteNow.

Ultimately, MacWrite was completed on schedule and shipped with the Macintosh. This left WriteNow in limbo until Jobs left Apple to form NeXT. WriteNow was owned by NeXT, and released for the Macintosh in 1985, published by T/Maker. Jobs approved of our design, and especially liked how we created the entire packaging from a single sheet of paper that folded into the box that would sit on a retail shelf.

Around this same time, many software companies that had only published software for the PC began expanding their offerings to include Macintosh. There was a group of Software Evangelists at Apple, led by Guy Kawasaki. In 1983, Kawasaki got a job at Apple through his Stanford roommate, Mike Boich. He was Apple's chief evangelist for four years. In this role, Guy's responsibility was to evangelize the Macintosh to anyone who wanted to increase productivity and creativity. In 1987 he was hired to lead ACIUS, the U.S. subsidiary of France-based ACI, which published an Apple database software system called 4th

Dimension. Mike Boich married Kathy Schlein, who worked a short stint at T/Maker, and was one of the Software Evangelists at Apple from 1983-1986. Another member of the Apple Evangelist Team was Alain Rossman.

Because of the early Macintosh work our design firm had done, we ended up doing work for Guy when he went to ACIUS, Mike Boich and Alain Rossman when they started a company called Radius, and Kathy's brother, Ted Schlein when he was at Symantec.

One of the most memorable events from this time period had nothing to do with software or computers. T/Maker had decided to host a party, first at their offices and then onto a movie theater on California Avenue in Palo Alto to celebrate the release of *Mad Max Beyond Thunderdome*, the 1985 Australian post-apocalyptic action film directed by George Miller and George Ogilvie and written by Miller and Terry Hayes. In this sequel to *Mad Max 2: The Road Warrior*, Max (Mel Gibson) is exiled into the desert by the ruthless ruler of Bartertown, Aunty Entity (Tina Turner), and there encounters an isolated cargo cult centered on a crashed Boeing 747 and its deceased captain. The film is the third installment in the *Mad Max* film series and the last with Gibson as Max Rockatansky. What made the party so unique was that everyone had to dress up as a *Mad Max* character. By far the best was Heidi's mom, who surprised everyone with a genuine dog collar around her neck and other leather accessories to round out the outfit.

Right up the street from our Palo Alto Office on University Ave was a little three person company that wanted us to design the packaging for their Macintosh version of a new software program called Quicken. Intuit was conceived by Scott Cook, whose prior work at Procter & Gamble helped him realize that personal computers would lend themselves as replacements for paper-and-pencil based personal accounting. On his quest to find a programmer he ended up running into Tom Proulx at Stanford. The first thing Scott did was to show me how difficult and how many steps it took to write and print a check with the other personal accounting software programs on the market. He then did it with Quicken. It was fast and simple. While we were working with Intuit, Scott asked if he could interview me about how I did my business accounting. We sat in a restaurant on University Ave. late in the afternoon and he peppered me with questions. Intuit was working on small business software that they were calling Quickbooks. He was curious to learn everything he could about how we did our books and to deeply understand the problems a business faced. Technology or software was never part of the conversation. It's a product lesson I've never forgotten, because he went right to the customer and asked questions to better understand the problem and look for ways to greatly improve the process from how it was currently being done.

The rapid growth of the software industry fueled the growth of my design firm and we soon had a team of eight people. As Stanford became a hotbed of software developers, my being in Palo Alto and also being aligned with Heidi and T/Maker kept the referrals coming in fast. It was about this time that I was approached by Bill Woodward who was getting his start as an entrepreneur. Fast forward to today, Bill is a successful entrepreneur and venture capital investor based in Southern California. He has founded multiple businesses in the technology space with over $3B of exits including Macromedia, Launch Media, MySpace, and many others. He has been an early/lead investor in a number of successful companies including Demand Media, Android, Spin Media, Beachmint, Blurb and various others. Back when we first met, Bill had discovered a talented programmer at Stanford named Young Harvill and needed help launching a new software company called Paracomp.

Young has a long list of high-tech accomplishments to his name. He has participated in the births of several influential Bay Area technology firms, with Paracomp being one of San Francisco's first multimedia companies—which was later acquired by Macromedia—and then Adobe. Ironically, I would end up working for all three companies during my career.

But when we got started, Harvill was a virtual reality (VR) pioneer. He co-created DataGlove, an early VR device, and invented Swivel

3D, one of the first modelers for the Macintosh in which a three-dimensional model is generated from a flat image.

Like Professor Don Knuth, Harvill, it turns out, is one of those rare souls who are able to nimbly navigate across the sometimes-wobbly bridge between science and art. And he focused on using light to convey three-dimensional space, and thus to create models that approximate life itself.

Paracomp attracted the attention of Jim Clark, who In 1982, along with several Stanford graduate students founded Silicon Graphics, Inc. (SGI).Jim would become a board member and early investor in Paracomp.

Harvill's interest in the fusion of visual arts and technology was formed early on. He learned to count and do arithmetic in binary code from his father, a one-time field engineer and computer operator for the company that made UNIVAC, the world's first commercial computer. He listened to his dad and his brother work out algorithms for solving problems, and often had opportunities to play on a computer, writing simple programs in Fortran. But his interest in the machine was only really piqued when it gained a rudimentary capability for generating graphics, which happened with the development of PLATO, an early computer-assisted instruction system that allowed users to plot lines of light.

His fascination with light in space prompted him to later study holography—a form of photography that uses laser light to record an image in three dimensions. He continued at Stanford University, where he earned a master of fine arts in 1984. He was later granted a fellowship from Stanford to further his work in printmaking and computer-controlled holography.

After graduating from Stanford, Harvill worked for a year with the Anderson Collection, one of the world's largest and finest private collections of 20th century American art. In his spare time, Harvill wrote the program for Swivel 3D, a software program for creating computer art, which gave users the ability to build interesting worlds on a Macintosh computer. He licensed the program to VPL Research, the first company to sell VR products.

In 1985 Harvill joined VPL, becoming the company's fourth employee. He worked on RB2 ("Reality Built for Two"), the first VR system, and co-invented the DataGlove, one of the world's first commercial VR products, which graced the October 1987 cover of Scientific American. Wired to a computer, the interactive DataGlove used fiber-optic bundles to discern hand movements and transmit the information to a computer, where the movements could be duplicated. The device made it possible to translate the wearer's gestures into manipulations of virtual objects, which has had applications in fields from gaming to remote-control surgery.

From there, Harvill went on to Paracomp in San Francisco and brought Swivel 3D with him. The company's products included design and visualization software targeted at such market niches as desktop publishing, industrial design, engineering, and film and video production. While he was there, he designed a new 3-D modeler, MacroModel. During its life cycle, MacroModel (later called Extreme 3D) was the most widely distributed multimedia modeler. Paracomp merged with Macromind to become Macromedia in 1991. In 2005, Adobe acquired Macromedia.

By this time we had learned how to successfully use the Macintosh as a design tool to not only present ideas to our clients, but also to do the actual art production, which in the past had been done by hand.

The majority of my clients were all located in Palo Alto or Mountain View and during this time very few software start-ups were located in San Francisco. The Paracomp office was on Townsend Street well before SOMA was a thing and the rents were some of the lowest in the entire Bay Area because of the undesirable location.

Our firm continued to grow and the amazing part was that all of our work was either from existing clients or referrals. In 1986, we had a call from a new company that had come out of Stanford and was on Willow Road in Menlo Park. The referral came from an early Intuit employee who had moved over to this new company. The founders were experimenting at Stanford University to connect detached networks in two separate buildings on campus. After running network cables between the two buildings, and connecting them with bridges and then routers, the two realized that to make the disparate networks talk to each other and share information, a technology was needed that could handle the different local area protocols. So they invented the multi-protocol router, which they launched in 1986. Most of our client base was made up of software companies, and this new client needed graphics for an upcoming trade show. When I first visited the offices, and the founders attempted to explain their product and what it did, I was at a total loss to understand the technology or purpose. We took the job, but I asked for 50% of the money upfront because I was skeptical that the company would make it. They offered to pay our fee in stock. I declined. How was I going to pay my bills with stock? Even their logo and branding needed work. It was orange with a bridge. The company was Cisco and if I had taken the stock, paying bills would have been the least of my worries.

We continued to work with new and interesting software companies. The best part was the various founders and their unique personalities. People like Bill and Ann Duvall, who had started Consulair, a software company out of their house in Portola Valley, a woodsy community in the hills above Palo Alto. Like the majority of my clients at the time, Bill & Ann were referrals and were looking for design and marketing help. What I didn't realize at the time was that Bill played a significant role in the history of the Internet, because on October 29, 1969 at 10:30PM, he received the first ARPANET message sharing digital information from a computer at UCLA to the computer he was sitting at in Menlo Park at Stanford Research Institute (SRI).

But it wasn't the software or technology that I remember about working with Bill & Ann. It was their lifestyle. They lived where they worked and were avid bike riders, working their schedule to make time for their passions and their family. Bill had pioneered remote work, when he suggested to SRI that he could program remotely from home in Sebastopol in Northern California. This was unheard of at the time. I watched as they built a company and a living, doing things unconventionally and with great passion.

Living Videotext was a software development company founded by Dave Winer in 1983. Its slogan was "We Make Shitty Software... With Bugs!," although the slogan was never publicly run in an ad. The company was founded to sell an outliner product called ThinkTank for the Apple II. After seeing a demo of Apple's near-release Macintosh, Winer hired his brother Peter Winer to develop a version of ThinkTank for the Macintosh, which by April 1985 had sold 30,000 copies, or to about 10% of all Mac owners. Work began on another outliner application at the end of 1984 called MORE, which expanded on the graphical concepts that they had started to add to ThinkTank, for example letting users easily convert outlines into bullet charts to be used in presentations. By 1986, the company grew to fifty people and released MORE for Macintosh, which our firm designed the packaging and advertising campaign. Before merging with Symantec, Winer first met with Bill Gates, the co-founder and then-President, CEO, and chair of Microsoft, in February 1987. Gates wrote a letter of intent to purchase the company in return for shares of Microsoft. However, the deal fell through and Microsoft instead purchased Living Videotext's competitor, Forethought, Inc., makers of Powerpoint, in a $14-million deal.

After receiving a number of other offers, Living Videotext merged with Symantec in September 1987. During this period of time all of the various Mac developers and software companies were working together to compete against the IBM PC and evangelize the benefits of the Mac. It was difficult, because the installed base of PCs was so large compared to the Macintosh, that it took courage to introduce software for the new Apple machine.

One thing that helped Apple was the introduction of Microsoft Word for the Macintosh on January 18, 1985. Bill Gates actually traveled to San Francisco later that year to accept an award from MacUser Magazine for Microsoft Word. My wife and I were at the event because a number of my clients were nominated for awards. Later that night we all went to the Redwood Room, The Clift Hotel's famous and historic bar on Geary Street. Heidi Roizen and the folks from T/Maker were there. Steve Jobs was there with Bill Gates and his girlfriend at the time, Ann Winblad. They met in 1984 at a Ben Rosen-Esther Dyson computer conference and dated for a few years. Even though they broke up after a few years, they remained friends. Ann would end up being the first investor in T/Maker later in 1989. She would also introduce me to a start-up called Aria Systems in San Francisco many years later that I'd end up working for.

Perhaps one of the best stories from this time period was when Heidi Roizen had a house guest in Menlo Park who happened to leave behind his American Express Card. T/Maker was in fund raising mode and was also on the radar of larger software companies as an acquisition target. She actually ran the credit card through the manual credit card machine at the office with the notation "One Software Company - Two Million Dollars" and returned the slip and the card to its owner, Bill Gates, in Seattle.

What I learned during these years from Heidi was something she acknowledged: "It's easier to get to know people when they're not famous; then when they do become famous, you already have a relationship with them." Roizen's willingness to invest time in developing relationships with people whom she simply found interesting and smart, as opposed to powerful - paid off repeatedly throughout the years.

While the majority of the work we did revolved around the Macintosh, we still worked on PC software as well. In 1985, T/Maker decided to broaden its product line and develop a user-friendly graphics package for the PC platform, an untapped market. Within months, the software industry was buzzing about T/Maker's impending product, named ClickArt Personal Publisher (Personal Publisher). We were hired to design the product packaging. The developer of Personal Publisher was Randy Adams and he had moved to California from the East Coast. Industry observers were hailing "sneak previews" of Personal Publisher as a "desktop publishing solution" for the PC. The market's widespread anticipation of the official product launch put significant pressure on the company to quickly finish the product. To speed up the process, the company diverted already short resources from the T/Maker product to Personal Publisher, causing Roizen's brother to become increasingly uncomfortable with the direction the company was taking. As a result, in 1986, Roizen and Farros agreed to buy out her brother's ownership stake for $500,000. In April 1986, Personal Publisher finally shipped, six months after the originally announced publication date. The company breathed a sigh of relief, but it was short-lived. Within days, market demand for the product was so strong that it swamped the company's operations. Realizing the company did not have the capital or staff to fully take advantage of the product's unique window of opportunity, Roizen and Farros decided to sell the Personal Publisher product to Software Publishing Corporation in late 1986.

Heidi and Royal continued bootstrapping until 1989, when it took venture capital from Hummer Winblad Venture Partners as their first venture investment. Ann Winblad became a director of the company at that time. Tim Draper of Draper Fisher led the company's second round in 1993 and also joined the board.

T/Maker was acquired in 1994 by Deluxe Corporation. Both Heidi and Royal left the company in 1996, Heidi becoming VP of Worldwide Developer Relations at Apple Computer and Royal founding and becoming CEO of an online print shop, iPrint.com.

After the success of Personal Publisher, Randy Adams would go on to start Emerald City Software and become a client of our design firm. The company developed and published PostScript language typographic products and development tools, among them the TypeAlign type styling program, the Smart Art collection of PostScript typographic and graphic effects, and Lasertalk Mac and Lasertalk PC PostScript. He sold the company to Adobe in 1990.

In 1990, I sold my design firm and went to work for Paracomp as Director of Marketing. Over the past six years I had learned first hand how hard it was to grow and maintain a business. Cash flow during our sudden growth spurts had almost put us out of business. It was counter-intuitive - we were growing like crazy, with great clients and we had no money. During this growth stage we had been doing work for Apple, unfortunately Apple loved the idea of stretching payments out 90 days from invoice. Many of the expenses associated with the Apple jobs were due before we got paid. Right when I started the design firm I had filled out an application for business school. I never sent it in and my wife, Jill and I ended up going out to dinner with the $50 application fee. Years later I would end up presenting at that business school to the students. Running a small business for six years was not easy, but the experience and the amazing people I was able to work with was priceless.

One of my clients, Steven Eichler, ended up marrying one of my employees, Judi Blaine. Steven Eichler had come to our firm with the idea of building community work spaces with computers and high-end furniture. It was WeWork, just with a 30 year head start. It was way ahead of its time, and never quite got traction. If you're from the Bay Area you may have recognized Steven's last name. His grandfather, Joe Eichler, between 1949 and 1966, built over 11,000 homes in nine communities in Northern California and homes in three communities in Southern California. Later, other firms worked with Eichler's company to build similar houses. Together, they all came to be known as Eichlers. During this period, Eichler became one of the nation's most influential builders of modern homes. The largest contiguous Eichler Homes development is "The Highlands" in San Mateo, built between 1956 and 1964.

Steven, who was 14 in 1974 when his grandfather died, remembers that "He had a booming voice, and was very much into politics, which at my age I didn't understand. He was definitely the patriarch, at the head of the table."

"I remember him being a big presence in the room. And I was impressed that he walked the talk. My wife Judi asked me, 'Did he live in his houses?' I said, absolutely. That's one thing I've always remembered."

"My finest memory might be of being in one of his homes he was living in. It was an area that was just being built and we walked through the subdivision. There were framing pieces, strands of electrical wire on the ground. It was absolutely fascinating to me."

About Joe Eichler's architectural legacy, Steven says, "I am proud of it. I'm very proud of it. It's cool and neat that he was my grandfather."

At the time that I took the job at Paracomp, we had begun a family and had a one-year old son, Brad. Part of the transition resulted from wanting more stability for my family and taking a break from being responsible for the business. I was also going to have to commute to San Francisco from Menlo Park, but I did have some flexibility and could take a train or drive.

Working at Paracomp was the perfect introduction to the inner workings of another venture backed software start-up. The majority of the team were in their late 20s, but we were lucky in that two of the early employees had parents who knew the inner workings of the emerging tech industry well. One of the product managers was Rix Kramlich, the other was Sean McKenna. Rix's father, Dick Kramlich, was co-founder of New Enterprise Associates (NEA), and has been in venture capital since 1969, when he joined Arthur Rock and Co. as a general partner. He was an early investor and board member of Paracomp. Sean's father, Regis McKenna, is a marketer who introduced many of the ideas that are now part of the mainstream in technology marketing. He and his firm were instrumental in the launch of some of the most innovative products of the computer age, including the first microprocessor for Intel Corporation, Apple's first personal computer, the first recombinant DNA genetically engineered product for Genentech, Inc., and the first retail computer store, The Byte Shop. Sean had started out in PR at Cunningham Communications and the offices were right across the hall from T/Maker. Bill Woodward had been visiting Heidi Roizen and also had a meeting with Andy Cunningham. In 1983, Cunningham moved to Silicon Valley, where she joined Regis McKenna and was immediately given project lead responsibilities to work with Steve Jobs for the launch of the Apple Macintosh. Sean and Bill got to talking about the new software company, and Sean realized he didn't belong in PR, but wanted to focus on the product side of the business and left to become a product manager at Paracomp. As Director of Marketing, I had a lot to learn, but the products, people and environment offered an incredible opportunity.

Shortly after I joined the company there was a great deal of pressure from our investors to grow the revenue and take a strong leadership role in the emerging graphics and multimedia software industry. As an individual company, Paracomp was not big enough or growing fast enough. We would end up merging Paracomp with MacroMind and then a third company, Authorware to ultimately form Macromedia in 1992.

Director, an interactive multimedia-authoring tool used to make presentations, animations, CD-ROMs, and information kiosks, served as Macromedia's flagship product until the mid-1990s. Authorware was Macromedia's principal product in the interactive learning market. As the Internet moved from a university research medium to a commercial network, Macromedia began working to web-enable its existing tools and develop new products like Dreamweaver. Macromedia created Shockwave, a Director-viewer plugin for web browsers. The first multimedia playback in Netscape's browser was a Director plug-in. Macromedia licensed Sun's Java Programming Language in October 1995. By 2002, Macromedia produced more than 20 products and had 30 offices in 13 different countries.

It was an intense and chaotic time trying to fit three different company cultures together, as well as integrate management teams, founder personalities and investor wishes. The person who brought things together was Tim Mott. Mott co-founded Electronic Arts, Macromedia, and Audible and held a variety of executive or board positions, or both, at each of those companies. While at the Xerox Palo Alto Research Center (PARC) in the 1970s, he was one of the first people to apply rigorous user testing to the design of user interfaces. But beyond his background in technology he had the rare capabilities required to build a strong profitable company.

We also had a strong product management team led by Scott Walchek. Brad Husick was another key product manager, especially in the early days, as he was the only product manager with Windows experience and responsibility. He ended up managing 17 products. I learned how important strong product management is to bring everything together, especially in a growing company, with an expanding product line.

Another key figure was Bud Colligan. In 1983, Colligan joined Apple Inc. as part of the team that launched the groundbreaking Macintosh personal computer. He later headed Apple's higher-education marketing group. As an early expert in education technology, in 1989, Colligan was recruited to be the CEO of Authorware, a computer-based learning software provider. In 1992, because of the merger of Authorware and MacroMind-Paracomp, he became CEO of Macromedia from 1992 to 1997 and took the company public on NASDAQ in December, 1993. During Colligan's tenure, Macromedia's annual revenues grew to more than $100 million. In 2005, Adobe Systems acquired Macromedia for $3.4 billion.

What the press releases and final outcome left out was the internal struggles and tension that existed between the different management teams and the founders Bill Woodward (Paracomp) and Marc Canter (MacroMind). I'll never forget at one of the early company all-hands as the three companies were coming together. Marc Canter raising his hand from the back of the room to ask a controversial question. A singer in childhood, Canter enrolled in Oberlin College intending to become an opera singer, and was exposed there to synthesizers, computer music, and building and coding computers. He asked his question with his booming voice and the entire room went silent. He would end up being forced out of the company in 1991. To make things even more interesting, Marc's wife, Devorah Canter, also worked at the company and would stay until 1994. I always got along well with both Marc and Bill Woodward, probably because of my background as a founder and former business owner. The new management team was trying to prepare Macromedia to go public and show a full year of consecutive profitable quarters to prepare for a successful offering. The new corporate style clashed with the scrappy entrepreneurs that had started the companies from scratch.

One of the other consequences of preparing for a public offering was to trim down expenses. As Director of Marketing, I had thought, naively, that my job was secure. But looking back our marketing department was probably over-staffed, especially because of the mergers and having to absorb people from all three of the companies. The work had been intense and never ending. It was the Fall of 1992, and Bud called me into a conference room and let me know that I was being laid-off. I was shocked and ill-prepared. I also was about to lose some of the early stock options that I had not vested yet. The good news was that I did have a share of pre-IPO options that had vested. With a bit of severance, and some vested options, I was out of a job and about to take a very long train ride for my commute home from San Francisco to Menlo Park.

Having spent so much time at Macromedia I had learned a great deal about multimedia and its potential. Having young kids, I was also aware of the opportunity to use computers as a fun, interactive, teaching tool. In 1992, Living Books began a series of interactive storybooks for children, first produced by Brøderbund Software and then spun off into a jointly owned subsidiary, which were distributed on CD-ROM for Mac OS and Microsoft Windows. The series began in February 1992 with the release of *Just Grandma and Me* in 1992 until it ended in 1998; other titles in the series included *Arthur's Teacher Trouble*, *Dr. Seuss*, and *Berenstain Bears* titles. Three titles exclusively created by Living Books included *Ruff's Bone*, *Harry and the Haunted House*, and a retelling of *The Tortoise and the Hare*. About this time I had collected a number of older children's books and had the idea to turn them into interactive books using some of the development tools that I had experienced at Macromedia. At this point I was ready to start over and try something new and I launched "Storybook Software" to produce interactive storybooks for kids.

I learned quickly that I didn't have the connections or the capital to license well known books like Living Books had done. What I did have was a collection of classic books that could be reproduced since the copyrights had long since expired. Through my Macromedia connections I knew a multimedia developer, Cathy Clarke, who agreed to do the programming. Royal Farros of T/Maker agreed to be a seed investor. The best part of the process of getting Royal to commit was that we walked around a square block of downtown Palo Alto numerous times and discussed the pros and cons of him investing the first funds. No slides, no computers, just the two of us walking and talking until we agreed on an outcome. This was an early lesson in how difficult and important getting that first investor to commit to a new company or concept is.

One of the things that we did early on was film a short video, showing my son Brad and my niece Megan interacting with the software in front of the computer. As we developed the product, I took a trip to New York City to meet with book publishers to see if I could license some children's books or interest them in becoming investors. My Aunt, Grace, had an apartment in Manhattan and I ended up staying there for the trip. I didn't make much progress and returned to California.

There was another design firm in Palo Alto during this time, called Publishing Power, that was owned by a husband and wife team, Judith and Michael Maurier and they had extra space in their downtown office that I could rent. It was above their office, sort of an attic space with no windows that you had to climb a narrow set of stairs to access. Judith and Michael had done a lot of work for Forethought, the company that developed PowerPoint and became part of Microsoft. During this time period they were working closely with the PowerPoint team to produce the manuals that were included with the software. I continued to look for investors to help finance the company. Someone had referred me to a local venture capitalist who had been a journalist. I remember him climbing up the stairs to visit my humble attic office to get a demo and pitch for the software we were building. He was polite and interested, but quickly told me that this was a "lifestyle business" and not something that fit his venture firm. He was absolutely right, I had started the business because of my kids and the current "lifestyle" I was experiencing. The best part is that he said "no" to investing really fast. Many less savvy VCs would lead on entrepreneurs with countless meetings and "next steps". Turns out the British venture capitalist and former journalist was Michael Moritz. Moritz works for Sequoia Capital and is a philanthropist and author of the first history of Apple Inc. Previously, Moritz was a staff writer at Time Magazine and a member of the board of directors of Google. Our paths would cross again and I would also end up pitching another company to Moritz in a much more formal setting many years later.

I was learning quickly that building a software company and raising money was very difficult and time consuming. On a personal level, my family was growing and my third son, Tim, would be born in May of 1993. It was time to figure out a way to get the company going or look for another way to make a living to support my growing family. The "lifestyle" software company for kids was not working.

There are critical times in the life of a business and it's really hard to decide at the time what the next step should be. You can talk to other entrepreneurs, you can confide in friends and family. But there are no "right" answers and the results of your decision won't be clear until much later.

Should I hold out, stay independent, and raise more money? Should I find a partner, sell the company, merge? Is it time to brush off my resume and look for a traditional job?

What would end up happening seemed at the time to be the best of both worlds. T/Maker would publish our children's CDs and help us expand our offerings and I would become General Manager of a group producing multimedia storybooks. Going from being independent to working within an established software company was not as easy or simple as it first appeared. I would need to fight for internal resources and funding for our products. But, I now had a steady income and the benefits of working for a company. We built a small team and went to work developing a series of titles and working with the Discovery Channel to make some of their children's content interactive.

During this time period, Bill Woodward, the original founder of Paracomp, had moved back to Los Angeles and had been working with one of the movie studios to turn their content into interactive digital products. He had approached our team to see if we would be able to do work with them. My wife and I actually drove to Los Angeles for a meeting with Bill and his team and I still remember changing out of my shorts and t-shirt in the parking garage below the office. This ended up being in direct conflict to the work we were doing for T/Maker. But we knew that T/Maker was in talks to be acquired and their focus was not on the interactive software we were building. After a tense meeting outside of the office at a restaurant in Palo Alto, we decided it was best to stay working with T/Maker and pass on the Los Angeles opportunity.

T/Maker was acquired in 1994 by Deluxe Corporation. Both Heidi and Royal left the company in 1996, Heidi becoming VP of Worldwide Developer Relations at Apple Computer and Royal founding and becoming CEO of an online print shop, iPrint.com.

T/Maker's remaining products were ultimately acquired by Broderbund, including the software my team was working on. It was time to do something new.

6

Chapter 5 - A Garage in Atherton

It was the Fall of 1993, and it was obvious that my time at T/Maker was short lived. At this time, Randy Adams was working for NeXT in Palo Alto on Deer Creek Road as Director of Engineering.

I remember Randy telling me the story of the "two Porsches" many years later. As part of selling his previous company to Adobe, he had bought a new Porsche. Steve Jobs also had a Porsche. In front of the Deer Creek Office, both Porsches would be parked right out front, with plenty of space in between. One day Randy was working and Steve quickly yelled at Randy that they "had to move the Porsches" because a potential investor from Texas was on his way to the office, and he would not appreciate the two Porsches and could potentially walk away from investing in NeXT. The investor was Ross Perot.

Perot initially invested $20 million in NeXT in exchange for 16% of the company. This was thought to be massively overvaluing NeXT. Moving the cars and getting the investment helped save Jobs' company. While he had a sizable personal fortune, Jobs couldn't afford to endlessly bankroll a company that was burning through cash.

Perot's faith in NeXT helped the company pick up further investments. Ultimately, NeXT never lived up to its potential. Its computers never sold like Jobs or Perot had thought. But it was an immensely significant part of Jobs' life. He learned skills at NeXT which helped transform him into the CEO who later turned Apple around. It was also at NeXT that Jobs oversaw the development of an OS which he later sold to Apple. Without Perot's investment and support, there's a chance that none of this ever happens.

Both Randy & I were at a point of looking for something new to do. Randy had realized from his work at NeXT that beginning in January of 1994, the Internet was going to be available to do commercial transactions and he sensed an opportunity. Internet Shopping Network (ISN) was born and we got to work in Randy's garage in Atherton, CA. I would be a co-founder working on sales and marketing. Randy would be CEO and the technical lead. Randy also had been successful in raising money and since he had sold a company, he had a track record of a positive "exit" that the venture folks liked. None of that mattered as we were way ahead of the market. We would end up pioneering much of what is taken for granted today in online commerce.

But first, we had to figure out what to sell. Randy was practical. He reasoned that anyone using the Internet in the early days would have a higher interest and trust in buying computer hardware and software, so we focused on offering these items. We scheduled meetings with two of the largest distributors of computer equipment, Ingram Micro and Merisel, Inc. to pitch them on our idea to create an online shopping site for computer software and hardware. We needed the ability to source the products and have them shipped directly to our customers. At the time Merisel had further expanded its operations by buying ComputerLand's retail franchise and distribution division for $80 million. There were more than 200 ComputerLand franchise locations across the United States, and the division had installed the largest number of local area networks (LANs) in the country. With the purchase, Merisel acquired the right to refranchise the ComputerLand name in the United States. The company operated as a separate entity from offices in Pleasanton, California. Unfortunately, Merisel was focused on traditional retail and saw little potential in our start-up idea. They were also operationally set-up to ship in bulk to the various retail locations. Letting them know that Ingram was interested didn't seem to help our cause.

At the same time we had reached out to Ingram Micro and had arranged a meeting with Greg Hawkins, a Sales VP, who, looking back, said this on his LinkedIn profile: "The most enjoyable and exciting time of my career was the time I spent at Ingram Micro. I was part of an amazing team that helped grow the business from $1 billion in sales to close to $30 billion. I was then recruited to become CEO of buy.com, a key player in the Internet/e-commerce boom of the late 90's, and I led the company's public offering in February 2000." Our meeting was set for the Fairmont Hotel in downtown San Jose. Who knows what would have happened if Greg had not been our champion or believed in the new online store we presented that day in San Jose.

Eventually we would travel to Santa Ana and visit their corporate offices, but having the first meeting in a neutral location played well, since it was convenient for Greg and we avoided the uncomfortable explanation of our working out of a garage (although it was a really nice garage, with air conditioning, finished walls and carpeting.) The meeting went well and we asked for the ability to sell all 30,000+ products that Ingram offered. We also mentioned that we were in conversations with Merisel and needed incredibly good pricing to be competitive selling online.

As luck would have it, when we visited Santa Ana, we learned that Ingram had recently updated their warehouse operations using robotics and the ability to pick and pack "high velocity" products so that individual items could be shipped out quickly as opposed to the usual method of shipping bulk pallets of goods to retail computer stores. This advancement, as well as our proximity to Stanford allowed us to install a fast T-1 connection to the backbone of the Internet and gave us two key pieces to make an online store work. There was still a lot to do, but we were beginning to see some potential. Randy told me to prepare for a "rocketship ride", and we were beginning to think that online shopping might actually have potential as a business.

In essence, our platform was able to relay orders directly from customers to Ingram Micro, which has the relationships with the manufacturer, and would use our delivery data to ship the items directly to the customer. As the business matured we were able to use the zip code of the order to trigger the shipment from the closest Ingram warehouse that had the item, if that location was out of stock, it would skip to the next closest warehouse until it could fulfill the order. We could check inventory, so we rarely ever listed anything that was not in stock.

The investment community had very different ideas. We visited Sand Hill Road and presented our pitch, only to be told that "Nobody wants to buy something on their computer. I can go to a store or use my phone and a catalog to buy things - it will never work." Even our first investor, Tim Draper, was a bit skeptical and ended up investing personally, not as part of his venture fund. When we needed more capital, his sister, Polly Draper, an actress, writer, producer, and director also invested. Everyone else we approached for money told us "no".

By now we had some capital, something to sell, and the infrastructure to begin to build our online store. We began by hosting the store on a NeXT computer and soon had to move to Sun Microsystem servers to handle the increased traffic. We reached a deal with Ingram and received CDs with their entire catalog of products and uploaded them and did a slight mark-up so that the pricing would be lower than what you'd see in a physical store or catalog.

In April of 1994 we attended a trade show with a small 10x10 booth in San Jose that was one of the first Internet shows and introduced the company and began promoting the concept for a launch later that summer. Back in the garage we had a monitor up on the wall that Randy had programmed to show how many visitors were in "our store" and how many orders and the amount of revenue that we were producing. In the beginning we'd end the day, together celebrating with a beer if we had any customers and revenue.

Randy and I believe that we were one of the first companies to sell goods on the Internet. Some say it was Pizza Hut (they started selling pizzas online in late August 1994) others say the actual credit goes to Dan Kohn, a 21-year-old entrepreneur who ran a website based in New Hampshire called NetMarket. On August 11, 1994, Kohn sold a CD of Sting's *Ten Summoner's Tales* album to a friend in Philadelphia, who used his credit card to spend $12.48, plus shipping costs. We don't agree with the NetMarket milestone. The Internet Shopping Network beat NetMarket by about a month, starting to sell our first items in July of 1994.

In order to take people's money we had to get creative. At this point no encryption existed yet to protect the credit card data we needed to get from the customer. Our first customers actually faxed their credit card information to us and we stored it next to a credit card merchant terminal connected to our system and we hand entered each card number for each order. Our customers used an email address and a password to access the store. When Verisign was founded in 1995 as a spin-off of the RSA Security certification services business, we were able to offer our customers the ability to securely enter their credit card information. We became one of Verisign's first customers.

To give you a sense of how skeptical people were to put their credit cards on the Internet during this time, I was invited to go on the Phil Donahue Show in New York in December of 1995, with a panel of bankers and other people starting to do business online, to discuss the safety of shopping online with a credit card. Donahue's shows typically involved some sort of conflict. The premise for this episode was that it was dangerous to put your financial information online and hackers would ultimately steal the information and do really bad things. Our job that day was to show that our new businesses could successfully take this information without any breaches and that we had the necessary security measures in place. I think the panel did a pretty good job and I always remember a quote from Scott McNealy, the Chief Executive of Sun Microsystems at the time, who said: "You think nothing of putting sensitive information in an envelope and putting it in a mailbox and the only protection you have is that you licked the envelope." Of course, online fraud would grow exponentially, as the amount of people moved online, but I'd still argue that the risks are no greater than those in the physical world, just different.

ISN and internet retailing as a category was gathering momentum and all of a sudden we were being asked for interviews and information from analysts and academics. Analysts like Forrester Research in Boston and various business schools from Harvard to MIT to Vanderbilt University had professors whose research was now focused on the Internet and the long term effect on retailing. Donna Hoffman was one of the first people to reach out to us. She co-founded and co-directed the first academic center for electronic commerce in the United States. Today she is a Professor of Marketing at The George Washington School of Business in Washington, D.C. Professor Hoffman is an internationally recognized academic expert and sought after industry speaker in the areas of social media, online consumer behavior, and digital marketing trends and has worked with major corporations on the topic of digital marketing strategy. She co-founded and co-directed the first academic center for electronic commerce in the United States. The New York Times calls her pioneering effort "one of the premiere research centers in the world for the study of electronic commerce" and the Wall Street Journal recognizes the effort as the "electronic commerce pioneer among business schools." The other professor was Erik Brynjolfsson, the Director of MIT's Initiative on the Digital Economy, *Schussel Family Professor of Management Science* at the MIT Sloan School, and research associate at the National Bureau of Economic Research. His research examines the effects of information technologies on business strategy, productivity and performance, digital commerce, and intangible assets. Both were pioneers that saw the early potential and invited us to come to their classes and interact with the graduate students who would soon be out in the marketplace.

Our growth continued and we had hired a PR firm and had been very successful in getting press for the new venture. The orders grew and we were shut down one day because we triggered the fraud alerts at our credit card processor because our sales volume had grown so quickly. We negotiated higher limits. But the growth was starting to put pressure on our capabilities to keep up with the demand. Our customer service consisted of Randy and I answering emails. Both of us had babies and young kids at this time, so we were able to answer emails almost 24x7, because we hardly had a chance to sleep, as one of our kids was keeping us awake.

We decided to look for a college intern to help. We interviewed a number of candidates, but the person that we ended up hiring, Kevin McKenzie, showed up at the garage in a suit and tie and was shocked when he found Randy and I wearing jeans and t-shirts. He had been coached by the Career Center at his college on what to expect for an interview, and we did not fit the stereotype of a growing start-up. He did end up taking the job and after two years at ISN he became one of the founding members of CNET.

We finally realized that it was time to move out of the garage and we found offices close by in Menlo Park, right next to SRI International, a well known think-tank that has been called the birthplace of some of Silicon Valley's most important innovations. The location gave us credibility and we were beginning to look like a real company, with real offices.

Besides offices, what we really needed was more server capacity and equipment to handle the demand we were seeing on our site. We had been talking to a sales person at Sun Microsystems and worked out a deal to list and sell their servers in trade for actual servers we could use in our offices. This saved us an incredible amount of our cash, but it also gave us capacity that few other companies had at the time. Much like the early Macintosh days, there was a tight knit community that was helping each other work on the Internet. Business people were still wary. How can you make money on the Web and the Internet? In a small office on Hamilton Ave. close to Cowper St. was Enterprise Integration Technologies (EIT) that later founded the CommerceNet consortium to encourage Web commerce, and worked hard on ways to do secure credit-card transactions. Dr. Jay M. ("Marty") Tenenbaum, was the person we turned to for help to accelerate business use of the Internet. While at CommerceNet, he co-founded Veo Systems (1997), the company that pioneered the use of XML for automating business-to-business transactions. Randy and I visit their offices and hire them to help get us up and running. Randy also gets contacted by a couple of students at Stanford who heard about our Sun servers and needed more capacity for their project called "Yahoo". We end up hosting Yahoo until they can get more servers of their own. Randy introduces Jerry Yang to Mike Moritz at Sequoia Capital and Sequoia ends up investing. We had pitched Pierre Lamond, another Sequoia partner, in the garage and he was not impressed with online commerce, and tells us as he leaves that he keeps his expensive cars in his garage and doesn't think this e-commerce thing will go anywhere.

In these early days, the first businesses to earn substantial profits on the Web are pornography and gambling sites. We actually joked with each other about starting a porn site, but knew that our wives would instantly shut us down or do worse things to us. Amazon and eBay have not yet started, and these two events will help to finally convince mainstream business to follow pioneers like us into online commerce.

There was another event that would help to begin to move e-commerce into the mainstream and give us the additional capital to continue to grow. One of the many issues we were facing was that computer retailing had historically low margins and we had purposely only marked up the majority of what we were selling about 3%, so that our pricing would stand out and be competitive. We had proved that we could sell online, but we hadn't proven it to be profitable yet. Right about this time we actually received an email from Michael Dell, with the subject line: "Are you selling anything?" Dell was first launched as a static online page in 1994 and by 1997 had become the first company to record $1 million dollars in sales online. By 2007, Fortune ranked Dell as the 34-th largest company in the Fortune 500 list. Randy and I had a lot to learn about selling computer hardware and software. We ended up hiring away one of the buyers from a local retailer, Fry Electronics, to help us.

We also had been approached by the Home Shopping Network (HSN) who had been working on their own version of e-commerce, headed by Jeff Gentry called HSN Interactive. HSN and Prodigy Services Company began working together on an online store to debut in the fall of 1994. Selling housewares, electronics, fashions, jewelry, and products for personal-computer users, the service was the first to use full-color photos rather than drawings of merchandise. In addition to the shopping aspects, the service also provided a bulletin board for contacting HSN hosts and celebrity guests. This internal group was not making progress as quickly as they had hoped and had seen what we had built at ISN back in April and were interested in working with us. HSN originated the electronic retailing industry in 1977. The idea materialized on a small AM radio station in Florida and had grown into a global MultiChannel retailer with worldwide consolidated sales of $2.2 billion in 2003 and a growing customer base of over 5 million. We were invited to visit their offices in Florida and quickly learned that they wanted to buy ISN.

Randy and I flew from California to St.Petersburg, Florida to visit the Home Shopping Network offices and meet with their management team. Jeff Gentry was our "sponsor" within HSN, but we also needed to meet with the CEO, Gerry Hogan, who had been an early executive for Ted Turner at Turner Broadcasting and had recently taken over at HSN. Then there was "Stella".

Jeff had warned us that in order for the deal to go through, we'd have to convince Stella, who managed the entire IT department consisting of 1000's of employees that managed all of the television shopping transactions, that the Internet was a viable channel to conduct business. She was skeptical. Over and over again we'd hear from other members of the HSN management team, "Stella isn't going to like this..." Randy and I wondered to ourselves, "why is everyone so afraid of Stella?". Turns out that Stella had built an incredible, expensive proprietary machine with equipment and people that we could quickly replace with the open and free Internet. No wonder she was skeptical. In the end we passed the onsite visit and moved on to having the HSN Mergers & Acquisitions Team come to Menlo Park to do its final due diligence before the formal deal was done.

The group from Home Shopping Network planned a visit to our Menlo Park offices and also a dinner in downtown Palo Alto at Il Fornaio Restaurant. Right before the visit we had just leased more office space and added desks and chairs to make us look bigger and even added signage. The first thing Jeff Gentry did was point to the sign and say something to the effect that "these guys are real" when in reality our value was in our software and not in our ability to lease office space or have a sign made. The other story was that one of the M&A Team members decided to light up a cigar on the patio at Il Fornaio, perhaps ok in Florida, but not ok in the Bay Area and the surrounding diners quickly made him put it out.

Turns out the lead acquisitions person from HSN was Peter Kern and this was his first introduction to an Internet company. Today, Peter serves as CEO, and Vice Chairman of the Board of Expedia. Peter, along with Barry Diller, had overseen Expedia Group's executive leadership team, managing day-to-day operations, since the departure of the Company's former Chief Executive Officer in December of 2019. After he left HSN, he founded Gemini Associates in 1996 and served as President from its inception through its merger with Alpine Capital in 2001.

The acquisition went through in September of 1994 and we agreed to stay on for two years as part of the deal. Little did we know what was ahead of us. Our arrangement was much like kids sent off to college. We were in California and our "corporate" parents were far away in Florida sending us money and giving us the freedom to do our own thing. One of the first things we did was expand our offerings from just computer products to other kinds of merchandise. We also were able to update the way we processed credit cards by using the HSN relationship with their payment processor (at the time they were one of the largest merchants taking "card not present" transactions) We also automated the way we communicated with our suppliers like Ingram by using "EDI" or Electronic data interchange, the concept of businesses electronically communicating information that was traditionally communicated on paper, such as purchase orders and invoices.

One of our biggest challenges was getting people to our "store" or web site. Advertising on the Internet was in its infancy and we experimented and tracked the effectiveness of each campaign. Unlike traditional media, we were finally able to get a sense of what was working and the actual acquisition cost of an individual customer. We were one of the first companies to try "banner advertising" and had been on the home page of Netscape when they launched their browser. We had negotiated to be on the home page, until the day Randy came screaming into my office to let me know that our ad was no longer showing on the Netscape home page. What had happened? Someone at Netscape, we never found out exactly who, had the bright idea to rotate the ads and get away from "static" placement so that all advertisers were guaranteed a set amount of impressions, based on what they were willing to pay. So in reality, we were getting the same amount of eyeballs looking at our ads, because of the growing Netscape traffic, even though we no longer had the security of seeing our ad everytime we visited the Netscape home page. Psychologically, we much preferred the static approach.

It was a constant time of experimentation and a new company called Netgravity was launched in 1995 and we became an early client. NetGravity, Inc. was later acquired by DoubleClick Inc.

The best part of being so early was that we were able to inexpensively test and experiment with a new marketing medium and get immediate results backed by data. We followed each transaction from the first click on our ad all the way to the shopping cart and payment. This basic flow is what Amazon used as the foundation for their incredible business.

One of the things that Randy and I realized early on was that we needed more technical talent to help grow the business. One of my former colleagues at Macromedia, David Kaiser, had introduced us to Boris Putanec as an early key technical hire. A serial entrepreneur by trade, Kaiser has been a founder at seven startups in his career including Navisoft, a Web server company that was acquired by AOL in 1994 and whose technology became AOLPress and AOLServer. In 1990, Kaiser was the first VP of Engineering at Macromedia, where we had worked together. Kaiser's department built a product line of more than 30 applications including Director, the seminal PC animation application and precursor to Flash. Previously, Kaiser was the Director of Projects for Informatics at the NASA Ames Research Center for thirteen years. The recommendation from David meant a great deal. In addition, Boris's recent background and education in computer science from Brown University, brought us unique early understandings of the Internet and its potential.

After ISN, Boris would go on to co-found Ariba Inc. (NASDAQ: ARBA) in September of 1996 and as a member of the executive team was responsible for commerce software technology and corporate strategy. He was instrumental in creating and driving the products that enabled Ariba to grow to a $250 million enterprise software company in only four years.

There was a cafe next to Kepler's Bookstore in Menlo Park and Boris and I sat outside as he described on a napkin the concept for a new company called "Ariba" and that he was leaving ISN. Perhaps one of the reasons he decided to leave is what happened earlier that Summer and the turmoil it caused at ISN.

Now that we were a part of Home Shopping Network, we had been asked to submit an annual plan and budget for the upcoming year. We decided that the best way to do this was to drive down to the Monterey Peninsula and have an all day off-site away from the office. We arranged to have a conference room at the local Hilton. The room we booked was a disaster. There were no windows and it was in the basement of the hotel. Randy announced that we were going to Highlands Inn instead. Highlands Inn is a luxury hotel in Carmel Highlands that overlooks the

Big Sur coastline and is rated one of the best hotels in Carmel, To make the day even more interesting, Randy received a call from Gerry Hogan, the CEO at Home Shopping, announcing that he was no longer CEO and the company had been purchased by Barry Diller. Our planning session turned into an extended lunch of confusion in the dining room of the Highlands Inn. We had no idea what was ahead of us with a new owner at HSN. In a move that was designed to advance his drive to build a new television network, media mogul Barry Diller announced that his Silver King Communications Inc. would buy Home Shopping Network Inc. in a stock swap worth $1.26 billion.

Diller, who built the Fox Broadcasting network for Rupert Murdoch, had plans to replace the Home Shopping programming that was running on Silver King's 12 UHF stations with a combination of local news and entertainment to create an alternative network. Home Shopping should not suffer a decline in coverage because it was widely distributed on cable.

We had no idea what Barry had planned for us. In the following weeks, it became clearer that Diller and his team would spend more time learning about e-commerce and visiting us in Palo Alto. Regular monthly meetings were scheduled and entire teams would visit our offices to quiz us on what we were learning.

Besides taking over Home Shopping Network, Barry had been spending time with fashion designer Diane von Fürstenberg, whose son had been interested in exploring new opportunities after graduating from Brown in 1993 and working as a trader for Allen and Company, a private investment bank in New York. Barry thought it would be a good idea if Alex spent some time researching and learning about ISN. As we learned more we soon realized that Alex was actually Prince Alexander von Fürstenberg, yes, a real prince. We also thought his real job was to keep an eye on us for his soon to be stepfather, Barry.

On his first visit to the west coast, Alex stayed at the Stanford Hotel in Menlo Park. It was close to our office and to downtown Palo Alto. It also backed up to the daily commuter railroad tracks that run from San

Francisco to San Jose. The first night of Alex's stay, somewhat jet lagged, he was jarred awake by what he thought was an earthquake and rushed out of the room, without his key, with little on, panicked, but glad that he was now in the lobby. The front desk quickly assured him that what he experienced was CalTrain and he could safely return to his room.

As he told us the story the next day, it made it easier to have the prince around the office. The monthly meetings with Diller were a little more difficult to manage. Looking back, Randy and I and the rest of our management team were dealing in a different league and we were losing focus on our core business, because we were spending so much time with the folks from Florida and New York. We also were going to miss out on the beginning of the crazy dotcom growth of online shopping companies that went public and watched the Nasdaq Composite stock market index rise 400% between 1995 and 2000, only to fall 78% from its peak by October 2002, giving up all its gains during the bubble.

In late 1996, we were prepared to spin out ISN and take it public and had started the process of talking to investment banks. We had hired Jim Cook, as our CFO from Intuit. It was also time to build a stronger management team and we were in the process of hiring Scott Randall, to be President and CEO from his job as General Manager at NECX Direct, an online computer products superstore, that had grown from zero to $35 million in sales. It would eventually be sold to Gateway for $100 million. Unfortunately, we had a couple of hiccups. First, Diller was against any kind of IPO, as he rightly suggested that the entire category was a "bubble" waiting to burst, and he would not be a part of it. Second, after hiring Scott Randall, NECX brought suit against Scott and ISN for breach of Scott's non-compete contract. Scott left and would go on to start Yahoo Shopping and FairMarket after his very short stint at ISN.

Both Randy and I had two year contracts with HSN and the end was in sight. We would both leave to start over at new ventures. ISN would fade into Home Shopping Network, but much of the monthly "internet" learning that Barry Diller and his team did in Palo Alto, resulted in what is now IAC (InterActiveCorp) a holding company that owns brands across 100 countries, mostly in media and Internet. The company is headquartered in New York City and includes properties such as Match.com, Tinder and Vimeo.

Randy would set-up shop in Downtown Palo Alto as CEO/Founder of Navitel, a consumer electronics company providing hardware and software consulting services to Microsoft and Compaq. I'd start a company called MediaFlex, close to home in Saratoga. We were both in for wild times. It was 1997 and the dotcom boom was just beginning.

From what I had learned at ISN, I was convinced that the internet could be used in new and different ways to do traditional tasks. The original idea behind MediaFlex was to be able to eliminate the need to pre-print physical items and instead only print them "on-demand" as needed and close to the person or company that needed the items. What if there was a digital library of images that could be searched and printed and then delivered directly to the customer? These capabilities are common today, but had not been available in 1997.

The original site that we built as a proof of concept sold high quality prints of art. A customer would find an image, choose a size and order the print to be delivered. The local US Post Office was across the street and I'd make the daily trip to send out the day's orders and chat with Linda behind the counter. We were using a large format HP Printer to print out the images and we had started to approach media companies to license their images to resell on the web.

Because of the experience at ISN, I was able to attract some early stage seed money to help get us started. One of the early investors was Pehong Chen, who had founded BroadVision in 1993 and had taken it public in 1996. We met at a lunch spot in Menlo Park and I gave him my pitch and he personally invested $50,000 and became one of our first board members. His company pioneered web-based e-commerce and was among the first to offer pre-integrated, packaged self-service web applications for process, commerce, portal and content management. ISN had been one of their early customers. The timing also benefited from the frothy interest in anything Internet related. Getting the first investor was always the hardest, and as new investors came on board, others soon followed. Just as important as having capital was the ability to attract the right people to help build the company.

I had been introduced to Bill Tobin who was at Sun Microsystems as a possible technical lead and he joined in early 1997 as our CTO. One of our early investors suggested we also talk to Anita Baker to help with business development and we had the beginnings of a small team.

One building over from us was a boutique venture capital firm called "Redleaf Venture Management" that had been founded by John Kohler who had been an early Netscape employee after stints at Silicon Graphics, Convergent and HP. John not only worked and lived in Saratoga, he was also an avid tennis player and we had an instructor friend Al Wong that we knew in common. My initial pitch to John was not in his office, but on the tennis court. I remember hearing similar stories from this time period about how many deals were initiated on soccer fields, baseball diamonds and other very informal settings. Living and working in the South Bay was definitely an advantage and having four kids in school and activities helped build my network and get the company off the ground.

At ISN, Randy had dealt with the investors, while I focused on marketing and product development, and I soon realized that I had a lot to learn and it was much tougher than I thought. As we added more investors the challenges would increase, and the really hard stuff happened well after the checks were cashed. Managing a board and investors was a full time job on top of trying to build a company.

One early stroke of luck was that we got noticed by HP, but not in the US, but in Barcelona, Spain. Barcelona was the base for the large format printing division of HP and it was expanding its product lines and looking for new ways to grow its business. From our web presence it appeared that we were much larger than our actual small Saratoga office. When the team from HP came to visit for the first time they thought they had the address wrong. They expected us to be in a large business park, not in a former suburban real estate office. The visit resulted in more printers, but more importantly a $500,000 market development commitment from HP to help us grow our business. The best part was that the deal was not an investment in the company, so we wouldn't be giving up any equity.

Working closely with the folks from HP was one of my first introductions to a very large company. Each meeting typically started with the senior HP person explaining their org and how things worked. At one meeting, our contact from the hardware side of the business whispered in my ear to pay attention to the "ink" guys, since they had "all the margin and all the money."

We quickly outgrew our small office in Saratoga and moved to Santa Clara, close to the University of Santa Clara. We continued to hire and began to raise even more capital from venture firms that were hungry to invest and wanted to see growth. Eventually we had HP join in as a corporate investor and suddenly we had angel investors, venture investors and a large corporate investor. But, be careful what you wish for, as I soon learned that managing all of the various interests of such a diverse group of investors was extremely difficult. As part of the most recent round of funding, the VCs had required us to hire a large law firm to replace Pete Marshall, the experienced start-up lawyer I had been using since we had started. The crazy part was that the new firm was not as well prepared to handle our business as our one person law firm was. Our account was assigned to a new associate just out of law school who was working around the clock, but who knew little about how to help us with our various legal needs. So we were paying more, getting less, all because our investors wanted us to work with a "name" Silicon Valley law firm. Ridiculous.

I actually really enjoyed working with the law associate and helping him learn more about the start-up process. I didn't enjoy paying such high fees and using our valuable capital in a way that didn't help build the value of the business.

We continued to grow and raise more capital and I soon realized that I was not the best person to continue as CEO and made the decision to step down as CEO and become Chairman and find management help. As the founder this wasn't an easy decision, but we had grown to over 100 employees and I wanted to bring in someone who had the experience and background to take us to the next level of growth. Dealing with our investors' expectations was starting to get out of control, I needed help. John Mackey, the founder of Whole Food Market probably has one of the best quotes I've ever heard about taking VC money. He founded his first Whole Foods store in Austin, Tex., in 1980 with a $10,000 loan from his father. The first store failed, but Mackey started over. By 1988 he had built a chain of five stores. Having exhausted the seed capital borrowed from family members and friends, he searched for venture capital to expand the business. "Venture capitalists are like hitchhikers with credit cards," he said. "As long as you take them where they want to go, they'll pay for the gas. If not, they take over the car and throw you out." I feared that I was on the verge of getting thrown out of the company I had started.

There was a seasoned executive who had spent many years at Fortune 500 companies like Apple in finance, that I knew through my father, because they both had worked together at Digital Equipment Corporation or DEC for short. He was semi-retired in Saratoga and available. My job was to convince him to join an Internet start-up as CEO. Ken Ratcliffe was an ideal choice. I had always worked in very small companies and had little experience with large corporations or venture investors. Finance was not my strength and the amount of capital we had raised was now in the multi millions and the company's value was growing past the $50 million mark. The expectations and stakes were high.

Ken quickly got to work and brought on Keith Fox, a former Apple and Cisco executive as a Board Member. Keith is currently the CEO of the Keith and Pamela Fox Family Foundation focused on children's health and education. His philanthropic work also includes a board seat at Lucille Packard Children's Hospital Foundation at Stanford. He also sits as an advisor to the Dean of the School of Business at the University of Connecticut. Keith has been an executive, founder, investor, and board member over his 30-year career. We couldn't have asked for a better or more qualified person to join our board at such a critical time.

Little did we know at the time but we were right in the beginning of the dot-com bubble when Ken started in 1999. He would stay on for 2 years when the dot-com bubble burst and

the company's value plummeted from $100 million to zero in a week, we had to lay off all employees and shutter the firm. The experience was "devastating" but Ken went on to use it as the inspiration for a novel he wrote in 2005 called "Manhook" about a tech start-up's CEO's wild ride through Silicon Valley during the internet boom.

Right after Ken had agreed to join, he also had been asked to become a board member at Draper Laboratory in Cambridge, Mass. As part of the process the Department of Defense (DOD) needed to do a background check and approve a security clearance for Ken. I ended up being one of his character references. Our office was still in Santa Clara and a DOD official showed up to ask questions, badge and all. I literally felt like I was in a spy novel. Turns out that The Charles Stark Draper Laboratory, Inc (the official name) was originally part of MIT and spun off in 1973. The primary focus of the laboratory's programs throughout its history has been the development and early application of advanced guidance, navigation, and control (GN&C) technologies to meet the needs of the US Department of Defense and NASA. The laboratory's achievements include the design and development of accurate and reliable guidance systems for undersea-launched ballistic missiles, as well as for the Apollo Guidance Computer that unfailingly guided the Apollo astronauts to the Moon and back safely to Earth. The laboratory contributed to the development of inertial sensors, software, and other systems for the GN&C of commercial and military aircraft, submarines, strategic and tactical missiles, spacecraft, and uncrewed vehicles. Much of the work is top secret. Ken ended up serving on the board from 1999 to 2008. Besides talking briefly before I had to do the reference interview, Ken never said a word about anything else during his time at Draper.

There has been much written about successful entrepreneurs in the Valley helping other entrepreneurs, and my experience reinforced this notion when building MediaFlex. Two of our earliest seed investors, besides Pehong, were Ed Jordan and Bob Downs, successful entrepreneurs who had sold their company to Cisco and started aggressively investing in start-ups in the late 1990s as seed investors. In contrast, we also had Venture money from a firm based in Seattle, Tredegar Investments, that had co-invested with Redleaf Ventures. The board member assigned to us was John Parkey, who had spent his early career at Microsoft as a product manager and had been the first PM for Microsoft Word. The good news is that we had many different investors with very different personalities and backgrounds, but that was the bad news as well. We had such diversity that it was difficult to get our board aligned and in sync - and this didn't even take into consideration the corporate investment from HP. It was a real mess that Ken had inherited and he would have to try and get some semblance of unity.

Meanwhile, so much money was flowing to Internet start-ups that there were now multiple companies competing in the print-on-demand/commercial printing space. Our monthly burn rate of cash had grown exponentially, but the actual revenue and sales was lagging far behind. This meant that we continued to need to raise more money to stay in business. Bubble economics was hard at work. It also had an eerie ripple effect. As we grew, we needed to hire more talent, especially engineers. Many companies were in the same situation, competing from a limited talent pool. It became so bad that we had recruiters who would help us find and hire an engineer, and then come back a month later and re-recruit that same person for another job (getting their commission each time and driving up salaries and compensation packages in the process).

Our VP of engineering had a solution that helped. We started outsourcing our software maintenance and bug fixes to a group in India (this was a novel and untested approach at the time). It worked well. We had a much more affordable way to get things done and we now had a 24/7 operation that allowed us to move faster. But it was still not enough. Ultimately our board wanted us to try and sell the company. HP had been the ideal target all along, especially since they had a seat on our board and an investment.

Everything changed in July 1999, when HP named Carly Fiorina chief executive officer, succeeding Lewis Platt and prevailing over the internal candidate Ann Livermore. *Fortune* magazine said of Fiorina's hiring as HP's first woman CEO that, "Carly Fiorina didn't just break the glass ceiling, she obliterated it, as the first woman to lead a FORTUNE 20 company."

From our perspective the hiring of a new CEO created chaos within HP, especially with the relationships we had built in the printing side of the business. Jerry Sonnenfeld, Writing in *Fortune* magazine in August 2015, described the hiring as the result of "a dysfunctional HP board committee, filled with its own poisoned politics, hired her with no CEO experience, nor interviews with the full board."

The support we had within HP disappeared as many of the key executives we had worked with left HP or retired. One of the most critical departures was Antonio Pérez who had spent 25 years working at Hewlett Packard; at the end of this time he was corporate vice president and a member of the company's executive council. In his career, Perez held a variety of positions in research and development, sales, manufacturing, marketing and management both in Europe and the United States. After leaving HP, he ended up at Kodak. Unfortunately his time at Kodak did not go well. Pérez was named one of the worst CEOs of 2011 by several online financial news sources and online publications. We will never know what might have happened if he and his team had stayed on at HP and built out a strong digital printing platform.

Not only had our support within HP eroded, but we needed to close another round of financing to stay in business. We had begun to get verbal commitments from our previous investors that they were willing to continue to invest. Naively, one of the things that we never counted on or even thought about was to plan for the "unexpected". In this case, one of our early investors, Ed Jordan, had committed to a $1M follow-on investment. His partner Bob Downs also would match this amount. Their commitments would solidify the commitments from the venture capital folks. Of course, nothing was for sure until all the paperwork was signed, and the money was in our bank account. Tragically, Ed, who had been on our board since the beginning of the company died suddenly. He had been one of our best supporters and advocates.

The day that I attended his funeral at St. Mary's Church in Los Gatos, CA, I also had to meet with our lead investors and work to finalize our upcoming financing. Without Ed's investment, the entire round was in jeopardy of falling apart and we'd be out of business. One of the most difficult things I have ever had to do was to meet with Ed's son, and ask him if he and his family would still be able to honor the commitment his dad had made. In the meantime, Bob Downs had visited our offices in Campbell, CA with a $1M check in hand, and since he was wearing shorts and a t-shirt was initially turned away by one of our employees who mistook him for a solicitor off the streets. Ed's family honored the commitment that their father had made and our investment round closed successfully. The difficult meeting took place at an Italian restaurant on Hamilton Ave. in Campbell with Ed's son, with the expectation that the family's investment would be delayed or canceled, not that it would go through as originally planned. Ed's family agreed to invest. We closed the round and were able to stay in business a little longer.

By now my role had changed significantly from that of the founder. As Chairman, I was doing my best to keep our investors, board, management team, employees and customers all on the same page and aligned on expectations. This was almost impossible given the environment in the Valley. Expectations were so high and unrealistic that no matter what we seemed to do as a company, more was expected of us, faster. Having money actually didn't help much, because the more we raised, the faster we were expected to spend it. It was a vicious circle that was not just happening to us, but was rampant throughout the Bay Area at the time. To make matters worse, there were at least four other companies that had become direct competitors of ours and who were all fighting for the same resources, customers and capital. The bubble was about to burst, not just for us, but for an entire industry that had been hyped to the max.

In February of 2001 we ceased operations and shut down the company. We did our best to salvage whatever value we had left and agreed to sell our assets to a company called printChannel.com in June of 2001. The press release issued by printChannel emphasized that the asset purchase helped fuel a new round of funding from Warburg, Pincus Equity Partners, L.P. "Before MediaFlex ceased operations, it had been developing leading-edge print procurement technology that is highly complementary to the proven printChannel solution. By merging the two technologies, printChannel.com will solidify its position as the print procurement platform of choice for print suppliers worldwide," states Oliver Pflug, CEO of printChannel.com. "We are particularly pleased that, as part of this purchase, Warburg, Pincus Equity Partners, L.P. has increased its financial commitment to making printChannel.com a long term industry partner." The technology purchased by printChannel.com will enable the creation of a supplier controlled network of print producers whose products form a single catalog accessible by corporate users. "Print suppliers will have the capability to address most procurement needs of their corporate customers through a single point of access. The ability to tie together multiple production locations, or supplier networks will be of particular interest to large printers, distributors, brokers and Facilities Management companies," said Pflug. As part of this purchase, printChannel.com has hired key members of the MediaFlex technical team.

But the story gets even more interesting. In the Fall of 2002, printChannel.com was acquired by Printcafe, a company based in Pittsburgh, PA. But wait, it gets even more interesting, as Printcafe became part of

BILL ROLLINSON

Electronics For Imaging, Inc (EFI) in February, 2003. I dug up an old fax from the same time frame in 2003, issued by Printcafe's accounting folks that issued a royalty payout to MediaFlex shareholders based on the sale. The amount was small. As the founder I had seen everything we had built disappear, but the one small positive outcome was that some amount of what we created ended up contributing to EFI, which today is leading the transformation from analog to digital imaging. Based in Silicon Valley, California with offices around the world, EFI continues to develop breakthrough technologies for the manufacturing of signage, packaging, textiles, ceramic tiles, and personalized documents, with a wide range of printers.

7

Chapter 6 - The Unfortunate Cake Disaster

What to do next? The company I had started was gone, and I needed something new to do. For a short period in the Fall of 2001 I worked back in downtown Palo Alto on the top floor of a three-story Victorian House crammed pack with lawyers and other random individual offices with a good friend, Sheldon (Shelly) Breiner, an investor and entrepreneur who was working on a number of ideas and had hired me to help him develop one of them.

I actually first met Shelly in Woodside, California in a parking lot next to Robert's Market early one Saturday morning. Turns out he was an avid runner and I had started running with a group loosely organized by our pastor at church, Bob Nicholas, every Tuesday, Thursday and Saturday morning, on the trails above Woodside in Huddart Park. I owe a great deal to Shelly and really appreciate him taking me under his wing in 2001 after we shut down MediaFlex. Many times we pay lip service to the importance of having mentors or listening to others who have gone and done what you're trying to do for the very first time. One of the very important lessons that I've learned as an entrepreneur is having the courage to ask for help and listen closely to someone who has experienced more than you and is willing to help. Shelly was one of those people.

He was born on Oct. 23, 1936, in Milwaukee to James and Fannie Breiner. His parents, Jewish immigrants from Eastern Europe, later moved the family to St. Louis, where they owned a bakery. One of my favorite "Shelly" stories was when he was working at his parents bakery and about to graduate from high school and go off to college. His parents wanted him to stay in St. Louis and work at the bakery and attend college close by. One weekend he was delivering a wedding cake that his mom had made and was cut-off and had to slam on the brakes suddenly. The cake did not survive. As he drove back to the bakery to tell his parents the bad news, he made the decision to attend Stanford and leave St. Louis behind.

The unfortunate cake disaster led to Shelly becoming a Silicon Valley serial entrepreneur, inventor and geophysicist. He took full advantage of his time at Stanford, earning a B.S., M.S., and Ph.D., all in Geophysics. Shelly recently died at the age of 82 and now I wish I had carefully listened to more of his stories and spent more time running the trails with him. He motivated me to run the Dipsea, a classic trail race in Marin County and numerous marathons. He not only loved to run (he had done at least ten marathons), he was an avid hiker, skier and photographer and traveled extensively to over one hundred countries.

On many of our trail runs together, he would abruptly stop and point out something interesting along the trail. He would also always have a great story to tell. The runs went quickly and I learned a great deal about building businesses and life in general. It's no wonder that Shelly was also an early member of the Peninsula Open Space Trust (POST), a non-profit organization helping people access nature for recreation and for their physical and mental health. POST works to protect lands that create a more connected network of regional trails and open spaces that can be enjoyed by all. Additionally, in collaboration with many public agency partners, they support opportunities to develop and improve public access amenities on those protected lands. Most of the trails we ran on were the result of POST.

At the time I joined him in 2001, he had established New Ventures West, his personal business incubator to conceive and launch high-tech start-ups. He was an idea machine. I was never quite sure what we would work on when I joined him each day. He had spent a majority of his career developing remote sensing to locate mineral and cultural resources through airborne, oceanographic and land based geophysical surveying and search techniques. In simpler terms, you could use an airplane or a boat and Shelly's magic instrumentation to find valuable stuff like oil. As a former consultant to various branches of the US government, Shelly was involved with detection of submarines, mines, tunnels, nuclear weapons and other ordnance. For example, he was involved in the search for two sunken U.S. submarines and a Soviet submarine in the Pacific and, at the request of the White House, he conceived and demonstrated, in 1968, the gun detector now the world standard for security at airports and buildings. On one of our many runs, he explained that he was a graduate student at Stanford working at Varian when he received the request from the White House after President Kennedy had been assassinated for a way to detect guns on a person before they entered a building. He set-up a make-shift lab in the hills behind Stanford and each week the government would ship a container full of guns to work with. With much trial and error, the result led to the metal detector that we all have grown so accustomed to walking through in airports and government buildings.

Probably the most memorable moment working with Shelly was when we took a trip to visit 3M in Minnesota and meet with Art Fry the inventor of the Post-It Note. Shelly had conceived a product to create digital Post-it Notes and wanted to show it to Art. The two inventors really hit it off and we ended up meeting at Art's house and eating homemade pie. Art retold a story that has been written about extensively, but hearing it first hand was refreshing and inspiring.

As a chemist at 3M he had been working on adhesives and one of his colleagues, Spencer Silver, mistakenly made one that didn't stick well. At the same time he had been singing in the church choir and the bookmarks that the group used to mark the songs they would sing constantly fell out during their performances. He had an idea - why not use the new "adhesive" to make notes that could mark the pages, but then easily be moved, since the adhesive wasn't permanent. Post-It Notes were born. Unfortunately, most people have only heard that part of the story. The best part was the rest of the story. To begin with, Art had an uphill battle to convince the folks at 3M that this was going to be a hit product. He went to the appropriate product managers and they were not interested, or had too much already on their plates to take immediate interest. Art didn't give up and his pure genius was what he did next. He had been making batches of the notes and handing them out to various employees at 3M. Demand was growing at a fast pace, and it was becoming a big job for Art to keep up, so he enlisted the help of the CEOs Executive Assistant to become the gatekeeper and order processor of the notes. When the assistant's productivity began to suffer because of all the orders, the CEO took notice and the result is what today is an annual run rate of $2 billion for Post-It and Sticky Note products.

What also struck me about the meeting was the childlike enthusiasm and curiosity that both Art and Shelly exhibited that day, even though both men were approaching the end of their respective careers and were well into their 60s.

The digital Post-It Note never quite got off the ground, but interestingly enough a similar concept is now a popular app some eighteen years later. Shelly was always way ahead of the times.

There was also a very low tech side to the weekly runs in Woodside. On Tuesday and Thursday mornings at 7am, I would meet Pastor, Bob Nicholas, Ross Edwards and Harry (the plumber) for a run on the trails of Woodside, ending at the Woodside Bakery. Some mornings we would mix it up and go to Edgewood Park in Redwood City, but that run missed the best part, the bakery at the end. The interesting thing was that Bob, Ross and Harry were all leaders of their organizations and were all exceptional entrepreneurs. None were in technology per se, but being located in the San Francisco Bay Area had a heavy influence on their individual work.

The issues and problems they discussed during our hour or so runs were important lessons and gave me a solid foundation as I was building my own business. The fact that they were all twenty years older than me also helped give me important perspectives. Like Shelly, they also had strong storytelling skills and incredible senses of humor.

The casual invitation to join this small running group would result in lifelong friendships and important lessons. I learned that Ross grew up in Columbus, Ohio, and all of his buddies were going to Ohio State, so he figured that he needed to get out of Columbus, otherwise it would be like an extension of high school. He decided that Purdue fit his criteria for civil engineering, and he always wanted to be in construction, so he enrolled at Purdue in 1956 and got his bachelor's degree in civil engineering in 1960. Then he met his wife, Gloria, at Purdue, and she had two more years in the School of Pharmacy, so he decided to stay on and get a master's degree in construction management and structures. So he finished that degree in January 1962 and left for California. After graduation, Ross thought he wanted to build bridges in Alaska and applied to four or five companies doing construction in Alaska and never got an offer. So from building bridges in Alaska to building buildings in Los Angeles was a step that he didn't anticipate, but it worked out pretty well. In 1971, he and Bill Wilson, Dave Boyd, and Miller Ream founded Webcor in San Mateo, California. The first letters of the founder's last names were used in addition to "co" for the "company" to form the name. The original logo was drawn by a member of Ross's church. For the entirety of their tenure, Ross Edwards and Dave Boyd would take turns being President and CEO.

In 1996, they would build Oracle World HQ in Redwood City, California - the company's first project with a high-profile, visible client. It was during this time period that we were doing our weekly runs and many of the conversations revolved around the current projects, especially Oracle. In the original plans, Larry Ellison, the founder of Oracle, was to have a first floor office. When the tower was under construction and Ellison saw the sweeping views of the bay and surrounding area from the top floor, the decision was quickly made to move his office there. In 2001, when Webcor celebrated their 30th year in business, the celebration was held in one of the Oracle buildings. Ross was a big fan of celebrations. Big and small. We were lucky enough to attend numerous events at their home.

There was one point in the history of Webcor when the economy had hit a major speedbump and all but one or their projects had been shut down. The one that remained was a public parking garage which had little or no profit. Ross said that most of the other construction companies had laid-off their workers, which seemed to make sense since there was no work. But the Webcor team took a different approach. They considered how difficult and time consuming it would be to get the best people back once things turned around again. So, although risky and counterintuitive, they continued to pay everyone. This one move turned out to be a major competitive advantage when the Valley turned around and there was a shortage of qualified workers. Not only was Webcor prepared, but they also had built up incredible loyalty so that it was much harder for competitors to poach their best people as business improved.

Another innovation was the idea of employee ownership and self-insurance. Webcor set-up the ability for their employees to own a piece of the company and have a vested interest. The same went for health insurance. They experimented with self-insurance, setting up a program where everyone contributed to the company pool. The incentive was to be smart about spending, since it was their own money at risk. The people always came first. Ross and Gloria lived out this philosophy in their personal life as well. I remember Ross saying he was meant "to serve" and that he did through his church and multiple charities and organizations he and Gloria continue to support.

Holt International is one of their favorites. It is a Christian organization committed to a world where every child has a loving and secure home. They help strengthen vulnerable families, care for orphans, and find adoptive families for kids. Ross and Gloria adopted their daughter Tami through Holt. Tami had been abandoned at a bus station in South Korea and ended up at an orphanage and because of Holt found her way to a loving family in Northern California.

As we weaved through the trails during those early mornings, Ross and Harry would often discuss the various jobs they were working on together. We all referred to Harry as "Harry the plumber" kiddingly, because actually he had built a very successful mechanical business that specialized in high rise construction - both plumbing and mechanical work. His firm, Design Mechanical in Redwood City, CA was also working on the Oracle buildings, as well as other large construction projects throughout the Bay Area. I was getting an education in an area that was totally different from the high tech environment that I was working in day-to-day. Listening to Ross and Harry go back and forth on the problems and opportunities of their businesses was inspiring. I also began to notice that they were starting to introduce computers and software into their businesses like never before.

Then to balance the construction and technology talk, we had the wisdom of Pastor Bob Nicholas to keep the rest of us balanced. He was also ultimately responsible for organizing our small weekly running club. On Saturday mornings, others would show up, but during the week it was only the four of us. Pastor Bob added a very interesting peak into the workings of a church and the challenges of being its leader. He had been called to Bethany Lutheran Church in Menlo Park a little before Jill & I started to attend. The church was part of the Missouri Synod, a traditional, confessional Lutheran denomination in the United States. Bob wasn't radical, but he had many ideas for the congregation that conflicted with the Synod. He also knew that implementing many of his ideas were critical to growing the congregation and attracting young families and keeping the church relevant in the changing Bay Area, so close to Stanford and the emerging high tech culture. It was a difficult struggle with no easy answers. Having members like

Ross & Gloria helped. Don Knuth, the Stanford professor and his wife, Jill, were also strong supporters and contributed much. Bob had also recently gone through a divorce and had remarried, another challenge he faced being the pastor of a traditional church.

The one additional thing that kept all of us grounded through the challenges of running our own businesses (and churches) was a good sense of humor and laughter. Despite the various ups and downs of life we continued to laugh and have some fun. Like the one time in San Francisco when Harry and some of the other folks at one of the job sites decided it would be a good idea to hoist Ross's Jeep with one of the massive cranes and leave it dangling by Moscone Center in San Francisco for when Ross finished a birthday dinner and went to find his car. Or the time when Ross replaced Harry's office chair with a toilet. Often when someone in town had a plumbing issue, they would always be encouraged to call Harry. With good humor, Harry would remind them, "I'm not that kind of plumber."

Soon after my brief time with Shelly at New Ventures West, Randy Adams and I would get together again to start another company with a third co-founder, Andy Jeffrey. AuctionDrop started in late 2001 and launched in 2002. The original concept was simple: "You drop it off, we sell it on eBay" The idea was to provide a platform for people who didn't want to hassle with listing and selling things on eBay to come to one of our drop off locations and have us do it for them for a commission. If the item didn't sell, we would return it to the customer or donate it to a charity. We started in San Carlos, CA with a small drop off location and a large open space to process the items that were dropped off. The business began to grow and we were able to raise some initial seed money from Tim Draper and then follow-on capital from Mobius Ventures.

Unlike the previous start-ups that I had been involved in, the one key difference with AuctioDrop was our dependence on finding and leasing real estate. We wanted to be in high visibility areas with high traffic to encourage people to drop off their stuff conveniently. We got lucky with our first location, since we had both a store front and adjacent space to process the goods. In fact we had leased a small amount of space, but the building we were in had not been partitioned off, so as we grew, we just creeped into the open space. When our landlord finally did an onsite visit, we realized that we had outgrown the space and needed to move. Ironically we ended up in Fremont, CA in the same location that had been the manufacturing facility for Steve Job's NeXT computer. We also were learning quickly about what merchandise sold well on eBay and the things that were bad. Since I was heading up our marketing and sales, my challenge was keeping the inventory coming in and the items selling through. Randy and Andy had written software to streamline the check-in process and the online auction listing components to help our items stand out and sell on eBay. We also quickly became aware of the high cost of doing this type of business in the Bay Area, our people and real estate overhead required to manage the items left little margin for profit.

We continued to expand and grow and add more drop off locations. Our relationship with eBay strengthened. We moved again, back to a new location in San Carlos that was larger and combined our offices and warehouse. We had five storefronts throughout the Bay Area.

Reselling designer goods became one of our strengths, but it also was a challenge as many items appeared to be genuine, but were fakes. Eventually we hired a team that had the expertise to spot authentic items that were valuable versus knock-offs that weren't and could jeopardize our reputation and status selling on eBay. Electronics also became another best selling category, but again required a good deal of quality inspection up-front to make sure we were selling working equipment.

As the growth continued and we were able to raise more capital, we added Ron Johnson to our Board at a time when we were expanding our retail drop-off locations. At the time Ron was heading-up the retail operation for Apple and had made an enormous impact introducing the Apple Stores. Randy and I had just signed a lease for a downtown store in Los Altos, California, convincing the owner that we were an acceptable risk. The owner's family had operated a pharmacy in the corner location and was willing to take a chance on us. As we planned for the build-out, originally we considered putting a sampling of the best auction merchandise in glass cases. Ron convinced us otherwise, and said he had gone through the same exercise at Apple and realized that people love to touch and see the merchandise up close and the risk of theft was actually a lot less then people speculated. In the long run, hiding and locking up the equipment had a much greater impact on killing sales, then the impact from theft. The Apple Stores continue to deliver and earn the highest revenues of any retailer on Earth - at more than $5,500 per square foot in 2017. Our Los Altos location, with the help and guidance from Ron became our top performing store. Years later my wife, Jill, took a job at the Apple Store in Los Gatos, CA. She was hired before the store actually opened to the public. On the day of the "grand opening", who decided to visit and see firsthand how customers reacted to the new store? Ron Johnson was on the floor, but not in any kind of official capacity, he was in shorts and a t-shirt having come from one of his kid's soccer practices and he was joined by his mom visiting from Minnesota. None of the Apple employees or any of the customers had any idea who he was. He was excited to show his mom what happened in one of the stores he and his team had designed. He was also looking for ways to make things better in the next location.

In the Summer of 2004, we decided that building-out our own individual stores was not scaling and we negotiated a deal to give us access to 3,400 UPS Store locations across the United States. A spokesman for UPS highlighted the benefits: "The benefit to UPS is the shipping revenue," he said. "But to the UPS Store franchisees, they get shipping revenue and packing revenue, plus it attracts more foot traffic to the stores." At this time, AuctionDrop had more than 24,000 items listed on eBay and had paid out more than $1.8 million to its customers.

But as good as the deal sounded, the economics behind the scenes were not improving. The cost to process the items exceeded the commissions we were receiving. The more volume we got, the worse the problem became. Our investors grew impatient and Randy and I were replaced with new management. Eventually the company was sold to ECO International, a business that helped retailers like Costco and Best Buy manage returns and the liquidation of electronic equipment.

I had learned a great deal about selling and marketing on eBay and had worked closely with Walt Duflock, who had been our relationship manager at eBay. He introduced me to Joe Campbell, who had built a small business in nearby Campbell, California to sell industrial equipment on eBay and was looking for some help. I was thrilled to find something new to do and take a break from working in a venture-backed start-up.

We had a small office and industrial warehouse on McGlincy Lane in Campbell and one employee, Jim, who helped with shipping and receiving items. With such low overhead, and much higher margins than AuctionDrop, JE Campbell was profitable and required no outside capital. What was missing was a steady flow of equipment to sell. My "sales" job became finding the right companies to work with to get access to equipment that would sell well on eBay and earn us reliable commissions. The focus on the industrial niche was fascinating. One of the companies that I ended up doing a great deal of work with was Applied Materials, the large semiconductor equipment manufacturer. Turned out they had a problem with excess inventory of spare parts used in large semiconductor fabrication operations and would take a quarterly financial hit if these items remained on their books. Our solution for them was simple. Not unlike AuctionDrop, we would list the spare parts on eBay and as we sold them, Applied was able to take the inventory off their books and get some revenue in return. A win-win for everyone involved. The other win for us was that the average equipment item sold for well over $10,000, and we had negotiated a 30% commission, so each sale was worth $3000.

We started to grow a reputation for certain types of semiconductor pumps that we're in high demand and that Applied had large inventories of. They sold through quickly. The only downside was that they were mostly located in a warehouse in Louisville, Kentucky and had to be shipped to California and then re-shipped to the purchaser. Many were in large crates and required a forklift for loading and unloading. The extra handling was not only affecting our margins, but also increasing the time it took to deliver and also increasing the likelihood of damage to the items.

It was time for a trip to Kentucky. We were able to convince Applied to "drop ship" the items we sold and totally streamlined the selling process so that it was completely digital. Just when everything seemed to be working smoothly we hit a big speed bump. Applied had been working on their own version of streamlining and had fixed their inventory problems and all of a sudden the majority of our best selling items were no longer available. Time to find some new customers.

We had been spoiled by the digital transformation of the majority of the business and just as suddenly we did a 360 degree reversal and signed a contract to liquidate the contents of a 500,000 sq ft. former Ross Stores distribution center in Newark, California.

A friend from my Palo Alto High days, David Thomas, was a Principal at LBA Realty and they had purchased the property that was still filled with conveyor equipment and a mezzanine that all needed to be removed from the property. It was a giant undertaking and we soon became a resource for selling conveyors of all types, as well as all of the other materials that were left in the warehouses and offices. Each day large semi trucks would leave with orders that we had sold on eBay. LBA wanted a clean, empty building to sell.

Somehow word got out to Merrill Brown, who had a company based in Hayward, California, that specialized in liquidating large industrial buildings. Merrill was closing in on his 90th birthday and worked harder and longer hours than anyone I had ever worked with. He would call the JE Campbell Office everyday to make sure we would give his company the work to clean out the Ross Location. He just wouldn't take no for an answer. His crew was from El Salvador and spoke little English, but would always answer any question with "no problem".

I quickly learned that there was actually a problem and what I had asked would not be easy to do.

Merrill's team worked just as hard as he did.

One morning I had stopped on my way to the job to grab coffee and a bagel. I thought of the crew and got enough for everyone. When Merrill showed up later in the morning he was livid. "What was I thinking?" he said. "You realize that now that you've done this once, the guys will expect it everyday!"

I learned a great deal from Merrill and his crew and the intricacies of dismantling and selling over a half-million square feet of warehouse equipment. Although our sales channel was eBay, everything else we touched was labor intensive and low tech and involved forklifts and semi trucks. We successfully cleared out the space and eventually the real estate became a FedEx Distribution Center.

Perhaps the best collaboration with Merrill came later when he got access to a closed Coca-Cola Bottling Facility in South San Francisco that had a number of room size, stainless steel tanks for making soda. What the heck, we put them up on eBay. Our expectations were low, and the back-up plan was to scrap them, if they didn't sell. Amazingly we got a hit from an entrepreneur who had just opened a new winery in Almaden, in the San Francisco South Bay. He needed the tanks for his new operation and we arranged to have them trucked from the old Coke facility down to the new winery. I'm sorry I never took up the invitation to go back and visit the winery once they were up and running, but I'll never forget those unique items finding a new home.

After spending so much time in warehouses and around forklifts and heavy equipment, it seemed like a time for a change. Selling industrial equipment was interesting, but not something that I was committed to doing long term. The economics of the business were also challenging, as our revenue was only as good as the timing and the items we could find to sell. No equipment, or the wrong item meant no sales. There was also personal pressure to find a job with more predictable income as we had three kids getting closer to college. I began looking for the next thing.

It was 2007 and I was soon to be unemployed. The lease on the office and warehouse in Campbell was done and I closed up shop. As I considered what to do next, I learned that Ross Edwards Jr., one of Ross Edward's sons, had decided to leave Webcor Construction, and form a new company called Build Group with a partner, Eric Horn (also from Webcor). Ross and Eric had extensive construction experience, but had never started a company before and they were hiring and looking for help growing their new business. One of the specific areas they wanted to concentrate on was to introduce a new innovative building approach using "pods" or pre-built structures that would be beneficial on large projects. "BuildPods" was born and this would end up being the area of the business that I was hired to develop.

This type of construction was already widely used in Asia and Europe, but had never caught on in the US and the timing seemed right, as computer aided design was growing and the ability to factory build complex items like bathrooms and kitchens in a controlled environment based on these computer plans, requiring less labor, resulting in a much more cost effective and faster outcome than building on site. Eric was passionate about the opportunity to change the way most building was done. Ross focused on building the traditional general contracting business that would be the foundation of Build Group.

As part of the hiring process, I also interviewed with Bob Simmons, a construction veteran, who had partnered with Ross and Eric to help them get established and round out the services they could offer customers. Bob owned a company called ConXtech. ConXtech was in the process of reinventing the way that structural steel-frame buildings are designed and built. Combining the tools of high-tech manufacturing with BIM (building information modeling), Bob developed an ingenious system of standardized components that make it possible to design and erect 2-to-12-story buildings faster, more safely, and with less waste. This type of construction was also beneficial in the Bay Area because of the various seismic zones and earthquake activity.

Bob also firmly believed in the Pods concept and was willing to offer space and resources in his Hayward factory to get the project off the ground.

When I started my job at Build Group, they had no formal offices and I began on-site at a project called Sunnyvale Town Center that was being developed by Peter Pau. I was acting as a sort of Project Manager and learning as much as I could about large construction projects, as we started to prepare to launch Build Pods. The time I would spend on the project was short lived and little did I know at the time all of the troubled history of this particular location.

The mall had originally opened in 1979 on a 36-acre sitebounded by Mathilda Avenue, Washington Avenue, Sunnyvale Avenue, and Iowa Avenue and comprising most of Sunnyvale's downtown, except for one block of its main street, Murphy Avenue. The City Council took the decision to build the mall in June 1976; demolition began in 1977 and included Sunnyvale Plaza, a twenty-year-old retail development.

The passage of Proposition 13 in 1978 reduced property taxes that the City of Sunnyvale had expected to use to pay off the bonds issued for construction of the Town Center, and also reduced interest rates paid by the developer. The fact that a third anchor tenant, JCPenney, was not obtained until 1992 further increased the city's difficulty in recouping the cost of the mall.

Over the years, the development went through a series of owners who either defaulted on loans or were sued for breach of contract. During that time, the mall fell into decline with changing tastes of shoppers and the emergence of newer and larger competitors. By 2002, the mall, then known as WAVE (Walking and Village Entertainment), was largely untenanted except for the three anchor stores, Macy's, Penney's, and Target, and the city decided to replace it with a modern version of a traditional downtown, including stores, restaurants, a movie theater, and high-rise apartment buildings. Redwood Square was to be a central plaza incorporating the redwood trees. Finally, in 2007, new entities named "Downtown Sunnyvale Mixed Use LLC" (DSMU) and "Downtown Sunnyvale Residential LLC" (DSR) took over the mall. DSMU and DSR were partnerships between Silicon Valley developer Peter Pau's Sand Hill Property Co. (which owned about 5%), and RREEF, a real-estate management business owned by Deutsche Bank (which owned the remaining 95%). The goal was to redevelop the mall into a high-end retail, residential and office development similar to San Jose's successful Santana Row.

Bob Simmons had proven his ConXtech technology at Santana Row after a massive fire destroyed the wood structure and the developer took a chance on the new steel construction to complete the project. Bob's concrete company had done all of the concrete work at Santana Row, so he already had a relationship with the developers and owners.

DSMU/DSR took out a loan of $108.8 million from Wachovia Bank; Wachovia was later acquired by Wells Fargo. By June 2009, with the mall demolished and Target having been replaced by a new store but the other new buildings incomplete, DSMU/DSR defaulted on the loan. Further development continued to be stymied by litigation between Pau and Wells Fargo. In May 2012, the City of Sunnyvale issued a press release accusing Pau of having filed "delaying lawsuits that have served little purpose other than to hold the project hostage",and claiming that "a nationally-recognized development team was set to come in and finish the project in 2011 ... until the barrage of lawsuits blocked their entry".In February 2013, further appeals were filed by both Pau and Wells Fargo; Pau's attorney estimated that the appeals would delay resolution of the case by at least two years. As of January 2015, apart from Target and Macy's the only active tenants on the site were Apple and Nokia, which have occupied new office space along Mathilda Ave.The remaining retail and entertainment space were still under construction and the residential units were all unfinished. The California Court of Appeals rejected Pau's two appeals in January and May 2015.Pau filed an appeal to the California Supreme Court,which declined to review the decision on August 12, 2015, effectively ending the litigation.On November 18, 2015, Wells Fargo announced that it intended to sell the mall to an ownership group made up of J.P. Morgan Asset Management, Sares Regis Group and Hunter Properties. That announcement triggered a 20-day review period during which the Sunnyvale City Council evaluated the proposed ownership group. On December 10, 2015, the Council voted to acknowledge that the new ownership group met the necessary criteria, effectively allowing the sale to proceed.

In July 2016, the city announced an updated agreement with the developer under which the project would be modified: some two-story retail buildings around Redwood Square, for which only the steel framing was erected, would no longer be built, but the project continues to include high-rise residential, restaurant, and retail components and a movie theater.In September 2016, the new development team closed escrow and took possession of the project,with a groundbreaking scheduled for October 2016. In October 2017, the city announced that AMC Theatres had agreed to lease the theater space for a 12-screen movie theater. In January 2019, Macy's announced that it would close its Sunnyvale Town Center store in March 2019, as part of a plan to close 8 stores nationwide.The store building had previously been sold; the site will be redeveloped as part of the rebranded CityLine Sunnyvale development, set to open in 2020.

As I write this, a global pandemic has wreaked havoc on retailers and companies like AMC. Who knows what the future of the project I worked on in 2007 will look like in 2021? What's amazing is that it is not anywhere near being finished.

Next the financial crisis of 2007-2008 hit. Not a great time to be starting a construction company. Luckily the majority of the jobs and work we were doing were not in housing, but in health care for organizations like Kaiser and Sutter Health. There were also projects that had already started and were fully financed and moving forward.

One of the highlights of working at Build Group was the opportunity to visit various sites to see projects under construction. We visited Rincon Center in San Francisco, when the South Tower, consisting of 376 condo units, was still under construction. We took the construction elevators to the top floor that was completely open, no windows, offering scary, but spectacular vistas of the surrounding bay. We were trying to convince the contractor to use the BuildPods bathrooms that we were selling. Unfortunately, The first residents began moving into the South Tower in February 2008 with traditionally built bathrooms.

Our concept resonated with architects and developers, but was a hard sell when it came to the general contractors and the various trades like carpenters, plumbers and electricians. It was my first experience with labor unions. They were not fans of our new technology and streamlined factory building process. Ironically, we thought we had that base covered as our factory was using Union Ironworkers to do all of our work. It was not enough and we continued to hit roadblocks caused by the various construction trade unions.

In doing our research, we learned that both Europe and Asia had a long and successful history of using this type of technology and construction. We entered into a partnership with a company based in Sweden and planned a trip to visit their factory in the northern town of Kalix. Eric Horn and I made the trip in early December via Stockholm, and then a short flight to an airport outside of Kalix. We expected it to be cold, but we didn't realize that we would also be dealing with a very limited amount of daylight, with the sun setting close to noon each winter day.

The factory building the bathroom and kitchen pods was fascinating and gave us a glimpse of what was possible and the amount of innovation and progress the Swedish company, Part, had made over their many years in business.

The company we visited began in 1989. The founder, Nils Lundholm, who at the time was running a construction company, had been commissioned to build a house in three weeks. The house had a timber structure and the customer wanted tiles in the bathroom. Since organic materials and tiles aren't a great combination, Nils and his team were challenged with finding a solution in a race against the clock. With time against them they hit upon the idea which, today, is the basis for Part. The solution was steel cassettes coated with plaster on the outside and lined with tiles on the inside. Pre-furnished bathrooms were lifted into place in the house, the water and power connected and the whole build completed within the prescribed time frame. The house was ready in three weeks. Nils realised that they were onto something with this new product that they had developed. Soon the company started supplying prefabricated bathrooms for hotel building projects in Sweden.

Then, at the start of the nineties, the financial crisis hit. Orders for houses were conspicuous by their absence, while the demand for bathrooms remained steady. The company mothballed its house production and the house factory became a bathroom factory. And with that, the new company Part was launched.

Nils also came to visit our factory in Hayward, California and we had planned a surprise for him. Turns out that he was an accomplished private pilot and loved to fly helicopters. Bob Simmons, the founder and CEO of ConXtech, happened to have a restored Huey helicopter at the airport in Hayward. The Huey or UH-1 became the first turbine-powered helicopter to enter military service in 1960 where, through the innovation and advancement of the capability, it revolutionized warfare. Shortly thereafter it was introduced to its iconic combat role in Vietnam.

This particular helicopter had been in Vietnam and the pilot who would fly us was a retired military pilot who had flown extensively in Vietnam. Our mission with Nils would be very different from what the helicopter had originally been used for. We had planned to let Nils take off from Hayward and then once we were airborne, we'd switch to the professional pilot who planned to fly us across the Bay, over San Francisco proper, and then dramatically under the Golden Gate Bridge, as we proceeded to Napa Valley for a lunch time meeting. The pilot let us know that he was not technically breaking any rules flying under the bridge, but that it was frowned upon, but he had made the necessary plans ahead of time so that we shouldn't encounter any issues. Being in the cabin that day and experiencing the breathtaking views with the chopper doors open was unbelievable.

As we headed north to Napa and landed at the Napa Airport, we all prepared for lunch to discuss the Pod business opportunities and how we could work together to bring Swedish innovation to the Bay Area. The spectacular ride that we all had just taken was a great way to get the day started.

Late in the day we returned to Hayward, after flying over the Napa Valley with the doors of the chopper open and wide angle views of the vineyards in every direction. It was an exceptional way to spend a day and also to get to know a new business partner.

Build Group continued to grow and moved offices after acquiring a smaller firm in San Francisco that specialized in interior construction for retail spaces. The Pod operation was moved to a back office and we finally decided that it was not going to make it as an ongoing venture. The challenges of working with the unions and the traditional trades like plumbers was too big of an obstacle to overcome. One of our early customers ended up being Vance Brown Construction at Stanford. We built an entire bathroom for an athletic field installation in the Hayward factory and trucked it to Palo Alto successfully.

I still vividly remember watching as the truck with the prebuilt structure turned the corner and arrived at Stanford. All of the meetings and proposals and pitches that went into actually getting a finished project installed successfully. Bittersweet as it was to shut down the operation, I'm glad that Build Group is thriving today and that they took a chance on doing something innovative in the construction business, even though it ultimately failed to take off.

Chapter 7 - Time for a Real Job

It was time to do something new and I was at a loss for what to do next. I had been out of high technology for the previous four years as I worked in the construction industry. I hadn't prepared a resume or really looked for a job in more than a decade. It was 2011, and the idea of starting another company didn't fit with the reality of three college bound kids. I needed to find a stable job in a growing industry.

One of our good friends, Bert Clement, had served as the CFO at Verisign and actually sat me down in his backyard and went through my old resume line by line and helped me revise it in a way that would appeal to a company looking to hire.

While I continued to look for a full time job, I ended up consulting at Symantec on a payments project for their eCommerce group. Starting Internet Shopping Network (ISN) and my work at AuctionDrop and JE Campbell had exposed me to online credit card payments and their growing importance as eCommerce was expanding. At the same time that we had started ISN in 1994, Bill McKiernan had started CyberSource to help merchants process credit cards online. On April 22, 2010, Visa agreed to acquire CyberSource for about $2 billion. Bill & I had become family friends as our kids had grown up together and attended the same schools. He was still working at CyberSource as part of the Visa acquisition and I let him know that I was looking for something new. I let him know that I was specifically looking for something in the payments space that would benefit from my entrepreneurial background. The outcome couldn't have been better and it's an important lesson to be very specific when asking for help. CyberSource had a group based in Boulder, Colorado, led by Dave Glaser that was called "Global Services" and worked on specific payments programs for larger enterprises and helped develop and manage new services and products that complimented the core credit card processing business. Global Services was looking for a Principal Product Manager to grow a billing service (the beginnings of the subscription billing services we are very familiar with today) With the combination of an introduction from Bill and the recent Symantec experience I was hired to work from Mountain View, CA for CyberSource, now a part of Visa. My job had a global scope and I had profit and loss responsibility for a new service that I needed to grow.

Working for Visa was a totally new experience from what I had been doing. There was an incredible amount of payment industry knowledge to learn, as well as figuring out how to navigate a much larger organization. Luckily I was part of a smaller, much more nibble team, primarily located in Boulder, Colorado. I also had the opportunity to manage two partner software companies that we were using to provide our main billing services. Unfortunately, one was located in Vancouver, Canada and the other was in Orlando, Florida. Geography was somewhat on my side, as Boulder was in-between, but this meant that almost 70% of my time was going to be on the road. Between visiting the two partners, meeting with my team in Boulder, and working with our global customers, I was headed for United Airlines 1K Premier Status in a record amount of time.

Not that it mattered much to me personally, but the CyberSource office in Mountain View was moved to Visa Headquarters in Foster City, CA. The CyberSource Mountain View location was taken over by Google and ironically when I was hired by Google in June of 2019, all of my training was in the building next door. Armed with my newly minted Google badge, I was able to go next door and walk around the old CyberSource office and try to locate the area I had worked in. Nothing appeared the same with the exception of the main entry area and stairs leading to the second floor.

My time at CyberSource and Visa gave me an incredible foundation in the payments industry and I was able to learn a great deal about e-commerce payments and the growing subscription payments trend. When I joined, the largest account using our billing service was Radio-Shack. Any customer who had purchased a cell phone and wanted a warranty was being billed monthly by RadioShack using our service. Unfortunately, RadioShack was not growing and would not be a long term customer. Back in our ISN days, Randy Adams and I had actually pitched RadioShack on setting up a substantial Internet presence to sell all of their electronics using the ISN backend. They declined our offer. It's been quite a ride for RadioShack over the past few years. The company first filed for bankruptcy in 2015, when General Wireless acquired the company. It filed for bankruptcy again in 2017, which led to many of its 1,500 stores being shut down. Today, some standalone stores in rural locations are still open. There's speculation that the brand may be reborn online in 2021? If only they had listened to us back in 1995.

What's surprising is that I spent a significant amount of my time evangelizing the benefits of companies changing their business models to support recurring business or a subscription model and moving away from one time transactions. Most of the companies we pitched didn't see the value or were unwilling to change the way they charged their customers. I would tag along with our enterprise sales executives on customer visits and explain what the new billing service had to offer. Quickly, I learned that these large customers were more concerned with fixing their ongoing credit card processing issues than adding a new service to their worries. The sales folks seemed to feel the same way, as the number of invitations I received to tag along to educate our existing enterprise customers on recurring billing had disappeared.

Not having much luck with our installed base of customers, I reached out to a brand new company called "Dollar Shave Club" to see how they were doing their billing. In their early days no one in the industry paid them much attention. Almost ten years later, I'm still a loyal customer and my credit card is charged each month, seamlessly, and my razor blades arrive each month in the mail. Dollar Shave Club was founded by Mark Levine and Michael Dubin. The pair met at a party and spoke of their frustrations with the cost of razor blades. With their own money and investments from start-up incubator Science Inc., they began operations in January 2011 and launched their website in April 2011, around the same time I started my job at CyberSource. They raised a fair amount of venture capital to grow the company, especially as customers like myself discovered the benefits of the service they offered. In 2016, Dollar Shave Club was acquired by Unilever for a reported $1 billion in cash.

The lesson here is that Gillette or Schick could have easily spun off a similar business taking advantage of the new billing services available on the Internet. They were the type of large CyberSource customers I was sitting in front of, explaining the possibilities of expanding their businesses and giving customers what they wanted. Unfortunately I was striking out both with our installed base and new prospects. Part of the problem was that we were early to market with a 3rd party solution that we were "white-labeling." In essence we were putting our name on a small Canadian company's billing software. We did add a number of new customers, but the sales cycle was incredibly long and we were way behind on making the original sales projections. The good news was that I was learning an incredible amount and meeting and working with some great people.

The one area that I especially enjoyed was learning about the payments happenings in the various emerging markets around the world. These were the countries and regions that didn't necessarily have the same kind of credit card penetration as North America and Europe. New payment methods were being developed, especially as it related to buying online. For example in Latin American countries, like Brazil, they have a method called "Boleto", that is unique to Brazil and allows a person without a bank account or a credit card to make an online purchase. Even when a customer has access to a credit card, often they are reluctant to use it online and only save the card for emergencies. Being able to better understand the various payment nuances in each of the countries, especially because of the global reach of my job was extremely valuable.

I traveled extensively. From Singapore to Australia, Japan and Europe. But for all I was learning, I also realized that working for a slow moving, bureaucratic organization the size of Visa was also not a great fit for me. Time to look for something new.

At least now when I was looking for a new job, I had relevant experience in a specific area of payments that was in demand. From my start-up days, I ended up reaching out to Ann Winblad, the co-founder of the venture capital firm Hummer Winblad Venture Partners. Soon my email was answered and Ann and I were on the phone catching-up. Again, I was specific about the kind of opportunity I was looking for and mentioned one of her portfolio companies, MuleSoft, and she instantly said that it wasn't right for me. But, she said, one of their portfolio companies, Aria Systems, was looking for a Product Manager for Payments. Aria has a sophisticated billing engine with customer management and marketing tools in a single piece of software. I took the job.

Another important lesson in getting into a company is that it never hurts to be referred by one of their investors. Looking back I don't even think the position was even posted or being recruited for. The new company and job was a much better fit than Visa, unfortunately the trade off I made had to do with my new commute in 2013, over 100 miles each day in the SF Bay Area, from my house in the South Bay to the Financial District of San Francisco.

At Visa, we had commuter buses to Foster City and back and if I did drive, I typically was traveling to the airport, not the office. I had learned how to work effectively on the road and without the benefit of an office or desk. Now I was back to much more of a regular routine, with little travel.

Driving to Aria was not a good option. Daily parking near our office was $35 and up for the day. And that was the price to pay after sitting in ugly traffic for over an hour and a half on a good day. The best alternative was Caltrain, especially the Express Trains, that skipped most stops and took a little under an hour to make it to San Francisco Station at Fourth and Townsend.

The problem was that it was still a good 20 minute walk from the station to my office on Market Street. And at night, the drive from the Sunnyvale Station to my house was another 30-40 minutes depending on the time I arrived. But I was determined to make the best of this new opportunity and quickly created a routine that helped make the commute a little bit more enjoyable.

First, I signed up for a commuter pass on Caltrain called a "Clipper Card", and was happy to learn that Aria would help subsidize a good portion of the monthly fee. Second, I joined the 24 Hour Fitness gym on Second Street, so that I had a place in between the Caltrain station and my Financial District office so that I was able to wear my running clothes on the train, stop at 24 Hour Fitness, take a run, shower and then go to work. I'd start my day by leaving my house at 5:45am, with a gym bag with work clothes, my backpack with laptop and work stuff, and I'd drive to the Sunnyvale station to catch the 6:13am express train to Fourth and Townsend. At a little after 7am the train would arrive in San Francisco and I'd walk the 15 minutes to 24 Hour Fitness and put my backpack and gym bag in a locker and then head to the Embarcadero along the waterfront for a run that took me up to Coit Tower on a series of steps that reached up from Battery Street. The run was about 4 miles and was a great way to start the day and experience the City.

On the stairs climbing to Coit Tower, the nearby houses hug the stairs, and it got to the point that the neighbors would wave as I went by. Once I reached the top of the hill and went around Coit Tower, I was always amazed each morning by the small group of mostly Chinese women who would be doing Tai chi, under Coit Tower, overlooking the Bay below. There would also be coyotes some mornings (one of the locals told me that tourists would often mistake them for dogs, because they didn't expect to see a coyote in the middle of a major city)

Once back at the gym, after showing and getting dressed it was a quick walk to my office. The evenings were a bit more of a challenge as I was constantly trying to make the express train. I ended up adding a scooter to my routine, so that I could shorten the walking time to and from the train and so I had a better chance of getting on the express train after work. Once I had the logistics of getting to and from work figured out, the actual work part was simpler. My role at Aria was working with all of our customers and all of the various payment processors to make sure the customers had access to the right type of payment methods globally to support their sales. My background from Visa was helpful, but in my new role I was getting a quick exposure to all of the relevant payment providers globally and working to make sure they were available on our billing platform. Gaining experience in subscription billing on a global scale with all of the different providers was going to turn out to be a very desirable skill set to have as this type of commerce continued to grow.

The challenge at Aria was that it was a small private company in a niche market trying to grow its enterprise customer base. Large enterprises tended to want to control their own destiny when it came to collecting money and were hesitant to outsource this key activity to a software as a service company. The sales cycle was incredibly long. The good news is that the switching cost was extremely high, so that once we had a customer, they almost never left. What was clear is that Aria was stuck somewhere in the middle. They were growing and had raised a large amount of venture money, over $180M to date, but they had not quite hit critical mass and would be more of an acquisition target, than an IPO candidate. When I left the company in 2016, they were on Series E, meaning that they had been through four previous financing rounds.

As an employee, this is not favorable to any equity compensation that might be offered, as all of the investors to date get first dibs on any upside. I had the opportunity to exercise a number of stock options. I chose to pass, as I never was able to get a straight answer on the current "Cap Table". The Capitalization Table outlines the ownership structure and how the various rights of stock that have been issued or promised to investors. Luckily from my start-up days I was familiar with what to look for and knew from personal experience that all stock is not created equal. Employees and founders typically get common stock, whereas investors get what's called "preferred" stock. Then, there is participating preferred stock, a type of preferred stock that gives the holder the right to receive additional dividends or value based on some predetermined condition. In many venture deals, the preferred stock may have a 3X right, which as my attorney once explained to me is like being at a poker table and winning your hand, but wait, the investor next to you also won, but has the right to get paid three times, before you get paid once. Yikes. Simply said, if a company like Aria got acquired for say $100M, and there was a lot of participating preferred stock in the mix, the entire $100M could be distributed, before the holders of common stock received any money.

The general public seems to always assume if you get stock options in a start-up, they will become valuable once there is some kind of exit event like a sale or IPO. It really depends on a lot of factors and isn't so simple. Having the ability to review and understand the company's detailed capitalization table and understanding the past financing structure can prevent unrealistic expectations and disappointment.

After almost three years of making the commute to San Francisco, I received a call from a recruiter at the software company, Adobe. They were recruiting for a payments product manager that had the subscription billing experience I had gained at Aria. Better yet, they were located close to my home in downtown San Jose. The commute had started to take its toll, despite breaking it up with my morning runs, and on occasional longer summer days, skipping the train and strapping my surfboard on the car and stopping early in the morning in Linda Mar Beach in Pacifica to surf before work. It was time to ditch the daily train rides and have a somewhat normal commute to an office close by.

For a short time, my son Tim also did the South Bay to San Francisco commute on the train. He lasted about 3 months, before he moved to San Francisco. One of his commute experiences was classic and unique for the Bay Area. After work he arrived at the train station and quickly realized that the trains had all stopped running (this happened occasionally when there was an accident or some kind of outage) When this happened, commuters would scrabble to get an Uber and that's exactly what Tim did with a couple of other riders that he didn't know. Because of the high demand for rides, Uber instituted their "surge pricing" which adds a premium to the normal fare. Turns out the strangers sharing Tim's Uber were software engineers working at Uber, one of whom, ironically had written the code for "surge pricing" As soon as they were underway, they told the driver that they updated their destination and were getting out in South San Francisco, and would be re-requesting the Uber, because they would be out of the "surge pricing" zone. Once they stopped, everyone got out of the Uber, waited a minute or so, and then got back in for the rest of the ride at the normal price.

Tim also had a scooter to help him get to and from the train station. His office was a bit deeper in the Financial District than mine, and he ended up having a couple of close calls on his scooter. Besides getting aggressively tapped in a crosswalk by a car, the worst incident was getting chased and bitten by a dog. No wonder he moved and ditched the wild commute after just a few months.

Leaving San Francisco was tough, I actually really enjoyed being in the City, I just didn't enjoy the time and effort it took to get there each day. The Bay Area infrastructure to handle traffic and its idea of public transit were well below par for what the area should be able to provide. I also watched first hand as the streets of San Francisco became littered with trash, people and poop. It was sad and unexplainable, as I watched some of the most talented people in the world go to their jobs surrounded by a crumbling City. I'd constantly read about the money and time being spent to clean up the problems, but each morning I'd see more broken glass from car windows that had been smashed and more people suffering in the streets in conditions that were continually getting worse. This was 2016. Fast forward to 2020 and the story is even worse. Individuals and businesses are leaving for cities like Austin, Texas. Some of this recent activity is due to the global pandemic caused by Covid-19, but the issues go much deeper and have been festering for many years.

The debate continues about the value of a location like the Bay Area to entrepreneurs and I believe there is a shift going on that will allow more diversity in both the type of companies built and where they are located going forward. The concentration of entrepreneurs will not be as pronounced in Silicon Valley going forward.

When I arrived at Adobe in 2016, I felt like I had come full circle from my graphic design days and my early days at Macromedia (On April 18, 2005, Adobe Systems announced an agreement to acquire Macromedia in a stock swap valued at approximately $3.4 billion). The big difference was that I was now in a Payments Product Management role that was heavily engineering focused. I would be the first hire to exclusively manage payments on the commerce platform at Adobe. The majority of the work to date had been performed by the treasury team and had an operational focus versus a strategic focus on optimization and performance. The successful growth of Adobe's subscription business model has greatly accelerated the need to focus on credit card billing and expanding payment choices for customers globally. As the numbers grew larger, the risk and the opportunity also grew to do more around the credit card transactions that provided a good portion of Adobe's revenues.

Being on the commerce team was a wonderful way to work with all of the various product groups within Adobe as well as engineering, legal, finance, treasury and support. Payments touched so many areas, especially as we began expanding our global footprint to include selling in the majority of the emerging market countries that were much more difficult to navigate from a payments perspective than North America or Europe. I was getting an incredible education, but as the single resource working across Adobe on payments I was also overwhelmed.

I loved the creative working environment at Adobe and the challenge of solving the various payments issues we were facing. My frustration was with my immediate manager, who constantly challenged our team to do more with less. He never seemed happy or satisfied with our work. It didn't help that we were an internal group that was understaffed and under-resourced. The engineering team we worked with when I started was shared across multiple teams, so it required re-educating on specific payment practices when we were assigned new team members.

I remember one of the conversations I had with my manager, when he asked why I hadn't made more progress on one of the initiatives I was working on. Explaining the issues I was facing, I let him know honestly that I didn't think I was the right person for the job I was in. Right about this time, Adobe had initiated a program that encouraged employees to explore transferring within the company to other positions. I knew that I wasn't going to improve my current situation, and I really wanted to stay at Adobe. So I started the process of looking for something new internally. It had been over two years since I had joined the commerce group and our team had grown from three product managers to eleven. In August of 2018 as I was exploring my options internally at Adobe I had a recruiter reach out from Google. They described the hiring process and I let them know that I was happy at Adobe and wasn't looking for a change. I was confident that I would be able to easily transfer internally, especially with all of the hype encouraging people to do it. There were literally signs posted around the building about the program and an in person session that I signed up for to get more information.

There was a job opening up in London that seemed a perfect fit for my skills and involved payments and commerce. The hiring manager was in San Jose and we met numerous times to discuss the role and he was very encouraging. My wife and I talked over the pros and cons of being expats and moving to the UK. We liked the idea.

The way the internal transfer worked is that in order to formally apply for a new position, you needed to complete an application online and wait. Taking this step also sent a message to your current manager letting them know that you had applied to another position within Adobe. Big mistake on my part. I was now in limbo on the London job and thought that I had a bit of an insurance policy as I also had identified a handful of other jobs that looked promising as backups.

It was now early 2019 and my manager confronted me about my desire to switch, brought in the HR department and let me know that I had a month to find something new within Adobe. I still had not received any word on the London job and one by one my back-up positions seemed to be going nowhere. The reality was that in less than a month I'd be out of a job.

I began the process of looking outside of Adobe and was lucky that a recruiter from Symantec had reached out about a payments position with a team I was familiar with. This resulted in a series of interviews and a verbal offer. In the meantime, a recruiter from Google called and wanted to know my interest in interviewing. Nothing was happening at Adobe, and the most frustrating part was that I wasn't getting clear answers, just more waiting with time ticking away.

To complicate matters a bit more, we had planned a family trip in May to visit our daughter, Anne, who was studying in Madrid, Spain. The plan was to have a new job all squared away, go on vacation with my family and come back to a brand new job. The day we were scheduled to fly to Spain, I was to receive the formal job offer from Symantec. As a backup and because I was curious to go through the process, I went through the formal Google interviews the week before I was to hear back from Symantec. Probably because I knew I already had a job offer, I was relaxed and looking forward to the five hours of Google interviews.

I arrived at the sprawling Google campus in Mountain View and signed in and waited. My first interview was in person with an engineering lead and would be technical in nature. The focus of the first interview was on how I would build a ticketing sales system and prevent payments fraud. There was a white board for me to show and explain how I would go about doing this. I had prepared by reading sections of a book by Eric Schmidt, Jonathan Rosenberg, and Alan Eagle, called "How Google Works". In addition I had listened to the last earnings call that Google had, paying attention to the questions that the analysts asked at the end of the call. Listening to the earnings call was something I had also done to prepare myself for the Symantec interviews.

In preparing, I was most concerned about the technical portions of the interviews I would face at Google. What I didn't realize at the time was that I was interviewing for a Product Manager position, but not necessarily a specific payments position. The group of people that interviewed me were from different product areas across Google, we spent little time talking about payments.

There were product managers from Cloud and Assistant product areas and one of the most memorable questions was the following. "So you arrive at the office and there's a note from Google's founders Sergey and Larry that they just made a deal with NASA to provide Gmail on Mars and it's your job to figure out the amount of storage space and latency that will be needed to provide such a service." This particular interview was via video, so the way I approached it was to ask a lot of questions, since I had no clue what the right answer was and ultimately I never really answered the question. First I asked what type of email content was going to be sent back and forth? How many typical users are online at the same time. What type of infrastructure existed to transfer data today (satellites, etc). What was the current latency and storage required for the existing customers using Gmail services to use as a baseline to calculate the needs for the new service. I'm glad I didn't try to give a specific answer.

What was helpful is that I had already gone through a series of interviews at Symantec and one of the engineers had asked me a similar question that you'd expect to get at Google: "How many golf balls can fit in a school bus?" So obviously this isn't the type of question they're looking for an exact answer to: it's more about how you work your way through it. Showing others how you think. So I start by guessing that a standard school bus is about 8ft wide by 6ft high by 20 feet long - this is based on the kind of school buses I remember from growing up. Obviously you could ask more questions, what specific type of school bus? In my bus example this means you have about 1000 cubic feet of space to fill. I calculate the volume of a golf ball to be about 2.5 cubic inches give or take. Divide that 2.5 cubic inches into the amount of space in the bus to fill and you come up with 660,000 golf balls. However, since there are seats in the bus taking up space and also given the spherical shape of a golf ball means there will be some empty space between them when stacked, I'd round down to maybe 560,000 golf balls? But I never gave an exact answer for this question. I also said another approach would be to do a sample section of the bus with 100 balls and then multiply to figure out what would fill the entire space, based on the sample. I learned in both of these interviews that giving the answer was secondary, the real purpose of these kinds of questions is to see how you approach problems and the way you think.

With the interviews behind me, and my last day at Adobe completed, I was in a holding pattern to move on to my next job. I had a verbal commitment from Symantec and was all set for the actual offer and to figure out my start date on the day we were scheduled to fly to Madrid, Spain for 10 days on vacation. The call with the recruiter and hiring manager was all set, but when I dialed in the Vice President that I also had interviewed with was on the phone. Turns out the CEO had resigned the previous Friday and a hiring freeze had been put in place. So while Symantec had every intention of hiring me, they couldn't commit to when they would be able to do it. The group suggested that it was probably in my best interest to take another job if it was available as they had no idea when the freeze would be lifted.

We flew to Spain. I was jobless, but I did have the time with my family to look forward to with no work related distractions for the first time in memory. Our plan was to start in Madrid and meet up with other members of our family and then drive to San Sebastián on the northern coast in the Basque region. Little did we know at the time that a year later the ability to make such a trip would be almost impossible due the global pandemic caused by Covid-19. But in May of 2019, Spain was spectacular and we met up with my daughter, Anne, her three brothers, Brad, Kevin and Tim and Kevin's wife, Morgan and Tim's wife, Olivia. My wife, Jill, also included her two sisters, Jayne and Julie, and their husbands, Mark and John. This type of trip was exactly what I needed to get my mind off of work.

We loaded a giant van with our luggage after a couple of nights staying in Madrid and six of us began our almost 5 hour drive to an Airbnb in the small town of Hernani located in the province of Gipuzkoa, Basque Autonomous Community, Spain. The town sits on the left bank of the Urumea river and is located about 9 km from San Sebastián. Originally we had a house reserved in the town of San Sebastián, but there was a mix-up with our billing and at the last minute, we were only to find something in the outskirts. We're so glad we did, as we had more room in the house to accommodate everyone and we got to experience a unique Basque town, with no tourists and literally no one who spoke english. There was a local bus close to the house that took us into San Sebastian.

Not only was the food incredible, it was affordable and the alleys full of restaurants seemed to be never ending with small incredible places to discover each day. People were everywhere, happy, laughing and talking between sips of wine and tasty snacks called *pintxos* (pronounced as "pinchos"). Invented in San Sebastian, the name translates as 'spike' or 'thorn' because this type of tapas is commonly served on the end of a cocktail stick. Great places we found to try pintxos include Borda Berri,

Atari Gastroteka, and Bar Txepetxa. It was easy to stay out well past midnight and not feel tired.

A few nights into our stay we had opted for a more formal sit down dinner and it was well past midnight as we were finishing our meal when I received a text from the US. It was Grace, the recruiter from Google requesting that I call her for some good news. My dilemma at the time was that I was really excited to talk with her, but I had consumed a fair amount of wine and was reluctant to do anything that might jeopardize my chances of working at Google. I made the call and found out that I had moved to the next step of the hiring process and a formal offer was being prepared. Grace knew I was on vacation and we planned to finish the process when I returned to the States.

Needless to say, the rest of the time in Spain was even more relaxing knowing that I had a job on my return. What's wild is that I didn't know at the time that the Hiring Committee at Google approves a candidate for a job, but the actual position is a mutual decision that is driven by the new hire as much as by the company. I would be a product manager, but the actual group that I would work for was still up in the air. Luckily I received some very good advice from a former Googler, Tracy Wilk, who had also worked in Product Management at CyberSource, to "follow the money" and to try and focus on opportunities in the Payments Platform Group at Google.

In June of 2019, I started my new job at Google, on the Payments Platform Team, working for Mark Walick, a former Apple payments team member who was well respected in the industry. When we returned from Spain, I actually had to decide between Symantec and Google, as the original hiring freeze at Symantec had been lifted and I received a formal offer for the position. Having the Symantec opportunity at the same time helped in my negotiations with Google, but I knew that Google was my first choice.

Starting the job at Google was nothing like I had ever experienced before in my work life. Although I was joining as the company was maturing with well over 100 thousand people, it still had the feel of a college campus and the energy of multiple start-ups all mixed together. My office location would be in Sunnyvale, but my training would be in nearby Mountain View close to the company's main campus. As I had mentioned earlier, I ended up taking part in a bike commuter program that offered an e-bike to use for 6 months. I also had access to the extensive bus fleet with wifi or I could always drive.

Then there was the food, and a gym with a great pool. When was I going to actually work?

Like an excited kid, my first couple of weeks I actually tried to do a little bit of everything because I didn't want to miss out on anything. In one of our training sessions we actually had a donut wall. The wall was wheeled in and there were different donuts on wooden rods. It was incredible. Of course people always talked about all the free food at Google and I never gave it much thought. But once it was actually a part of the work routine it started to make a lot more sense. It was much more than just a place to eat, it was a great way to get to know your colleagues in an informal setting outside of the office or a conference room. You would also meet up with people you might not see or work with on a daily basis. It also kept you close to work, with really no reason to leave the Google Campus.

About 9 months into my new job at Google, in late March of 2020, everything changed. A global pandemic hit hard and our offices closed. As it stands in early January 2021, we are not scheduled to return to our offices until September, 2021 and that will be with a hybrid work schedule that has us physically in the office for 3 days and at home or remote for the other 2 days of the week. It will be interesting to see how this policy evolves over time, given that many other tech companies like Microsoft, Facebook and Twitter are allowing remote work with no restrictions.

No one knows for sure what the office will look like going forward. I miss my colleagues and the interaction that being together is a shared workspace encourages. It is definitely a time for experimentation and an open mind.

9

Chapter 8 - The Great Relocation

In early Summer of 2020, we decided to relocate from the San Francisco Bay Area to Raleigh, North Carolina. Little did we know at the time that we would be part of a much bigger trend that is continuing into 2021. People have started to refer to the period we're currently in as "the great reshuffling." Our reasons for going South had a number of factors, with family being first on the list. Three of our four kids were in the Raleigh area. We also purchased a home in the Historic Oakwood section of Downtown Raleigh in 2017 as an investment and a possible place to live when we retired. When Covid-19 hit, it gave us an opportunity to rethink our plans and priorities.

Over the past few months, each day brings a new story about a company or individuals relocating. The Wall Street Journal featured an opinion piece on November 15, 2020 by Joe Lonsdale, moving his venture firm and family from Silicon Valley to Austin. It was thoughtful and well written and I sent Joe an email to thank him for his thoughts. He responded quickly and gave me the go ahead to use his experience in this book. The bottom line for Joe was that bad policy has made California unlivable, so he moved his family and his venture-capital firm to Texas.

In addition, Hewlett-Packard, Oracle and Tesla have all announced their plans to move their headquarters out of the Valley. In the past years,

I had personally experienced the shift start-ups made from the Palo Alto area to San Francisco. Now I believe that the ability to start and grow a thriving business is not as dependent on the physical location as it once was. I'm currently working with a start-up based in Florida that is thriving and doesn't need to be located in a tech center to attract the necessary talent or capital to grow. The Raleigh area that I've relocated to has a vibrant start-up community anchored by the three Universities close by: North Carolina State, UNC at Chapel Hill and Duke. Covid has also made the idea of working remotely more of a mainstream idea. Time will tell, but we definitely are seeing an incredible shift in not only the way we work, but where we choose to work.

Having spent the majority of my life in Silicon Valley, the switch to North Carolina has been refreshing. The Raleigh area reminds me of the Palo Alto I grew up in the 1970's. The pace is slower and the area is heavily influenced by the nearby universities and colleges. The nearby Research Triangle reminds me of the Stanford Research Park. The Stanford Industrial Park, as it was first called in 1951, was the brainchild of Stanford University's Provost and Dean of Engineering, Frederick Terman, who saw the potential of a University-affiliated business park that focused on research and development and generated income for the University and community.

On NC State's Centennial Campus, **there is a mixture of corporate, government and not-for-profit organizations. In order to lease space on the property, a prospective "partner" must have some programmatic connection to NC State, such as collaborative research with a faculty member or the use of students for internships or part-time work. Currently, about one-third of the partners are start-up or early stage companies, many located in Centennial's co-working incubator, Raleigh Founded. Another 20% are research and development units of large corporations and the rest are small businesses, state and federal agencies, and nonprofits.**

As part of my move to the area I've started working with the team at NC State focused on Entrepreneurship. NC State has a complete infrastructure of academic programs, faculty talent, cutting-edge tools, investor networks and institutional support, including a tech transfer office that's among the best in the nation.

It's my contention that Silicon Valley isn't going away, but it is changing and the talent and capital it once dominated control over is spreading out and landing in places like Austin, Denver, Miami, Raleigh and beyond. While some argue that the Bay Area has been irreparably damaged by remote work, alongside alleged government hostility toward the industry, others think this death knell is overblown.

Silicon Valley, and the greater Bay Area in general, has always attracted entrepreneurs and pioneers, going back to the early days of the western expansion of the United States. And it will for the foreseeable future. But there are a few factors at play that we haven't seen before -- a global pandemic starting in 2020, global climate change that's turning the best weather in the country into fire storms; declining prestige for once best-in-class public higher education; crumbling transportation infrastructure; and an unprecedented wage gap across the region. Remote workers, tax refugees, that's the easy stuff to weather. There probably won't be a "next Silicon Valley" anywhere else, but the incredible Silicon Valley I experienced first hand won't exist either if some things don't change. I, for one, wasn't willing to hang around any longer to see how things turn out in the future.

10

Chapter 9 - Another Startup?

"Better to start something imperfectly than to do nothing perfectly."

Even though I've made the transition from entrepreneurship to working for a large company, I've continued to have the desire to start and work on something of my own. Back in 2017, I started a small side project called Surfitlocker to provide a way to rent outdoor equipment, specifically paddle boards in a self-serve way using a mobile phone.

I originally got the idea when I was working for Visa and traveling a great deal for my job. Often I would run early in the morning before work in the various cities I visited. But there were many times when I was in Florida or Southern California or Australia or Vancouver, Canada, that I'd want to rent equipment so that I could go surf or paddle board early in the morning when the conditions were the best and I wasn't yet required in the office. It was near impossible. I could go the day before, but I had no easy way to transport the equipment or an easy way to return what I rented. While I was thinking about this, I noticed some of the first bike share installations in Boulder, Colorado and London, England and tried them out. This was almost ten years ago.

The best part of working on a side business is that for the first time in my entrepreneurial life, it is not my sole source of income. The other advantage is that there isn't the intense time pressure to bring a product or service to market quickly to meet outside investor goals. What it has reminded me, over and over again, is that starting a new business is incredibly hard and humbling, even with decades of experience. But it is what I love to do.

The other incredible part of the process is the people you get to meet along the way and get to work closely with. So far, Surfitlocker has been a financial bust. Our first location in Monterey, CA was launched successfully, but we quickly learned that the location was cold, foggy, windy and downright dangerous. But it was a start. Our second location in Petaluma, CA did a little better, but our partner lost their lease on the marina location and our technology wasn't quite ready for a full scale operation that could scale. Back to the drawing board.

Then a global pandemic hit, which was actually a positive for the outdoor industry, but now my day job was demanding the majority of my time. Time to rethink the entire business. Luckily I have the patience and the luxury to take a step back and start over.

First thing I did towards the end of 2020 was to reach out to Padl, a company with a similar business plan based in Florida that had grown to five locations and was a full time operation, not a side business. I offered to help any way possible and started to work out a partnership to manage their locations outside of Florida in 2021, specifically in North Carolina.

Working with Andres, the co-founder and CEO we identified a number of targets that we expect to close later in 2021. Surfitlocker would outsource all hardware components like docking stations and equipment to Padl and focus only on providing software as a service to rental locations that wanted to manage and rent their own equipment.

The current expectation is that we will have the next round of our software available in the Summer of 2022 and will be back in business again.

Chapter 10 - Lessons Learned

Perhaps the best lesson that I have learned to date is that it is really important to follow your own unique path. No matter how much you read, listen or learn from other entrepreneurs and mentors, your journey will be different. For some, the rise to business success is a long, painful process. Many fail. For others, everything just seems to work. There is no magic formula. What is important to focus on is to develop an ongoing curiosity and an appetite to continue to learn and adapt.

The following is a recap of the 9 simple lessons every entrepreneur should consider in order to build a long-term, healthy and sustainable business.

1. Location still matters. Would I still recommend starting a company in Silicon Valley? It really depends. Today there are many more options that just didn't exist a few years ago. Yesterday I saw this quote on Twitter from Brian Chesky, the founder of Airbnb: "*Yup, the place to be was Silicon Valley. It feels like now the place to be is the internet (which is everywhere). I expect this trend to only accelerate*"

2. Hire and work with people who are smarter than you. There will always be people who are smarter than you. If you're lucky enough to find these people, hire them and more importantly work with them. Focus on the things that you're best at, and give them the freedom to do the same. One of the great pleasures I've had both in my own companies and working at Google is the opportunity to work side-by-side with incredible people.

3. Find partners. Building companies and products is hard. Having reliable partners not only helps you share the incredible workload, it can also significantly reduce the time it takes to launch. The best partners offer skills and expertise that you lack or just don't like doing. This is a lesson I wished I learned a lot earlier in my career.

4. Embrace design, marketing and sales. Perhaps I'm biased because I spent the early part of my career focused on design and marketing, but I often hear from business owners that spending money up front on design and marketing services is "too expensive." The truth is, skimping on design and marketing can make your brand look cheap.

Sales is also another discipline that often gets overlooked, especially by technically driven companies that think their products are so good that they don't need talented sales folks.

5. Not all money is created equal. This was one of the hardest lessons for me to learn. It was especially hard when I had payroll due and a pile of bills to pay. This is another instance when a simple "no" will save you from falling into the trap of taking money from anyone who offers it. There are investors and clients that are just not worth it in the long run and can hinder your future attempts in attracting capital. Much better to avoid this "problem money" as early as possible.

Be ready to fire a client or customer. There are clients and customers who take up too much of your time, who consistently have unrealistic expectations or who you just generally dread working with. Just say "no"!

6. Know when to say "no". I still remember Dave Kaiser, the VP of Engineering at Macromedia pulling me aside when I was Director of Marketing and telling me simply - "Bill, you need to say "no" more often." He was right, I was trying to please too many people and trying to do too many things at once, many of them things that really didn't matter. I should have simply stood up and said "no".

7. Focus on time, not money. Often people tell me they don't have enough time to do something important. Money, clients, customers, ideas: are all resources you can potentially gain more of. However, time is a commodity you'll always have a set amount of. One way to ensure you make the most of your time is to prioritize how you spend your time and make sure to schedule all of your important tasks. This is when saying "no" becomes even more important.

Running has always been an important part of my daily routine. When Jill and I were in the middle of raising 4 kids, there never seemed to be a good time to go "run". I attempted to do it after work or at lunch. It never worked. Then I realized that if I started at 5:20am, I'd be back home before 7:00am, before anyone had gotten up. This is a routine that I kept for over twenty years. The other important part of this lesson is that I didn't do it alone. Rain or shine, I knew that there were others waiting for me, so it was much harder to skip or make an excuse not to show up. You have to make time for the things that are important to you.

8. Be humble and have a sense of humor. We all tend to take ourselves too seriously, which is why I'm such a huge fan of taking a humble and humorous approach to work and building companies. When you're passionate about what you do, and when you focus on happiness and approach problems with a smile and curiosity, work isn't just something you do to fund your "real life." It becomes infinitely more enjoyable and meaningful, and significantly reduces your chances of experiencing burnout. I've learned over time that my favorite entrepreneurs are fun to be around and don't take themselves too seriously.

9. Start something and keep it simple. Planning, strategizing and weighing all the options have important roles for a business. But there comes a point in time when you just have to start something. The best business ideas tend to take complicated problems and solve them in simple ways that can be explained easily. Don't get stuck worrying about getting everything right before beginning. Many of the things that we needed to launch the Internet Shopping Network in 1994 didn't exist when we started. We didn't wait.

A closing thought. **Be curious and ask the three "Whys".** I'm not sure exactly what podcast I heard this lesson on, but it is something that I always try to do more of. The premise is that the more you probe by asking "why?" the better understanding you get of what the problem you're trying to solve is. But, you don't ask the "why" question once, but three consecutive times. Trying each time to get a deeper understanding of why what you're doing is important. It is a good way to avoid getting caught up in doing what others tell you is the "best way" to do something. Problem is, "they" don't know *your* customers or clients the way you do. Use "why?" as a starting point, to make sure you're focused on the unique needs of your business and your customers.

12

Acknowledgments

To my wife, Jill, for encouraging and supporting me through the ups and downs of entrepreneurship and working in Silicon Valley.

One of the first people I reached out to for help on this book was Micheal Malone. When my wife and I were first married, her boss, J. Peter Nelson, introduced us to Mike and I remember him giving me a copy of one of his first books, *The Big Score*, and how much it influenced my passion for building businesses and working with entrepreneurs. Malone worked in public relations for Hewlett-Packard Co. before joining the *San Jose Mercury-News* in 1979. Malone is the author of 15 books, covering the world of business and technology, including *Infinite Loop: How Apple, the World's Most Insanely Great Computer Company, Went Insane*, *The Big Score*, *The Virtual Corporation* and *Intellectual Capital*, *Going Public*, *Virtual Selling*, and *One Digital Day*.

The second person I need to thank and acknowledge is Alison Carpenter Davis, who recently wrote her first book, *Letters Home from Stanford: 125 Years of Correspondence from Students of Stanford University*. The book is a fun collection of the handwritten and electronic correspondence of generations of Stanford students. Since this was my first attempt at writing, I wanted to get Al's perspective and thoughts on the process and experience that she had just been through.

Sean McKenna for helping me remember what the early days at Paracomp were like and telling me the story of how he originally got hired as a software product manager and moved from PR (being Regis McKenna's son and working in PR had its challenges) to working as a senior technology executive who helped launch a wide range of technology products including 3D modeling software, network-centric video surveillance solutions, 3D motion tracking devices, alcohol-based fuel cell systems, and consumer and professional applications. Recently he has been involved in numerous social entrepreneurship projects at Santa Clara University.

Delly Tamer, who I worked with at Internet Shopping Network and went on to be one of the early employees at Netflix and now is the founder and CEO of Biztera in the San Francisco Bay Area.

Philippe Bouissou, the author of *Aligning the Dots,* who I first met when I was at Internet Shopping Network when he was at Apple managing e-commerce. He is an accomplished entrepreneur, CEO, venture capitalist, and board member with thirty years in Silicon Valley growing and running businesses. Currently he is Managing Partner at Blue Dots Partners LLC, a management consulting firm focused on top-line revenue acceleration for companies or business units with revenues between $10 million and $1 billion.

13

About the Author

Bill Rollinson worked as a Product Manager at Google. He has lived in Silicon Valley the majority of his life and helped to create some of the first software for the Apple Macintosh in 1984 and co-founded the first online retailer on the web, Internet Shopping Network in 1994. He's been involved in numerous start-ups, as an operating executive, founder, investor, and board member. He received a Design degree from UCLA. He has four grown children and currently lives in Raleigh, North Carolina with his wife, Jill.

www.ingramcontent.com/pod-product-compliance
Lightning Source LLC
LaVergne TN
LVHW010343070526
838199LV00065B/5777